INSPIRED *to* KNIT

CREATING EXQUISITE HANDKNITS

michele rose orne

INTERWEAVE PRESS.
interweavebooks.com

Technical editing: Lori Gayle

Fashion illustrations: Michele Rose Orne

Technical illustrations: Gayle Ford

Text © 2008 Interweave Press LLC

Photography © 2008 Interweave Press LLC

 Interweave Press LLC

201 East Fourth Street

Loveland, CO 80537-5655 USA

interweavebooks.com

Printed in China by Asia Pacific Offset

Library of Congress Cataloging-in-Publication Data

Orne, Michele Rose, 1963-

  Inspired to knit : creating exquisite handknits / Michele Rose Orne, author.

    p. cm.

  Includes index.

  ISBN 978-1-59668-041-8 (pbk.)

  1. Knitting. 2. Knitting--Patterns. I. Title.

  TT820.O654 2008

  746.43'2--dc22

                    2007036776

10 9 8 7 6 5 4 3 2 1

to jack, katherine, james, and andrew—
FOLLOW YOUR DREAMS! YOU CAN DO ANYTHING
IN LIFE IF YOU SET YOUR MIND TO IT!

Turning this book into a reality has been a long-standing goal of mine and bringing the concept to life depended on the work and support of many others.

To my husband, Matt, and our children Jack, Katherine, James, and Andrew—thanks for your love, support, and understanding of my many late nights sitting at the computer and my bringing along knitting wherever we went. Thanks for eating at the kitchen counter for more than a year while the dining-room table was covered with "knitting stuff" and for putting up with a wife and mother who is "always knitting."

To my friends—thanks for all your encouragement and support!

To my wonderful and considerably talented knitters—thank you for taking so much care in helping to develop these patterns and for all your patient efforts and willingness to work through the inevitable flaws of the initial designs: Grace Beverly, Ann Dill, Lucinda Heller, Anne McLaughlin, Jeanne Moran, Aloisia Pollack, Karen Ressel, Alison Walsh, Donna Warnell, and Kelly Young.

To my knitting industry friends who supplied yarns, information, and support: Pam Allen, Elaine Eskesen, Pat Chew, Nancy Thomas, Margery Winter, Veronik Avery, Susan Mills, Linda Niemeyer, Helene Rush, Kirstin Muench, Judith Shangold, and Linda Braley.

To the editors and staff at Interweave: It was a pleasure to work with such an accomplished team—from the initial creative brainstorming all the way through the technical editing, your encouragement, patience, and support were invaluable! It's been a pleasure to have such talent help bring my vision to life.

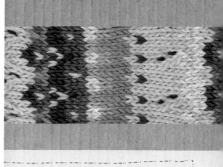

introduction
INSPIRED *to* KNIT

Where does inspiration come from? Those who create often look to the world around them for inspiration—to the work of other artists, to nature, and to their own creative spirits to come up with new expressions. They find new ways to interpret what they see and reinvent it in their chosen medium. My medium is knitting. Just as a painter uses paint and a sculptor uses clay, I create with yarn.

If you're like many knitters, choosing a pattern and yarn may provide more than enough challenge. How, then, can you learn to think more creatively—to make adjustments to an existing pattern or design your own? Knitters are often beholden to the written pattern—to exactly what appears on the page. Gripped by the fear of making a mistake and handicapped by a lack of knowledge about the basic concepts that go into creating a pattern, they're at the mercy of designs and patterns that others have created. I want to show you how—even if you have no design experience—you can find inspiration in your surroundings and translate that inspiration into your own knitting.

For this book, I've developed four short workshops to help you find inspiration and shape that inspiration into your own garments. Through these workshops, I'll guide you in gathering ideas, developing a color palette, knitting swatches, and sketching a silhouette for your own inspired projects. Along the way, you'll learn how I used these steps to develop four collections of projects that follow seasonal themes.

Although I make a living as a designer, I've never taken a single knitting or knitwear design class. My approach has evolved over twenty-five years of designing and knitting both professionally and personally, and it's based on a lot of trial and error. And I still make mistakes and rip out my work—sometimes entire sweaters that haven't turned out as I hoped. And I often alter my designs "midstream," if the knitted stitches don't behave as I envisioned. I tell you this so you'll know that it's okay to make mistakes and try new things. If you don't, you'll miss out on a lot of exciting design opportunities.

I've provided a wide range of projects in this book because I know that different types of knitting appeal to different knitters. Some are drawn to single-color projects, some to cables, some to lace, and some to color work. Depending on where your comfort lies, some projects may seem daunting. My intention, however, isn't to overwhelm you with techniques and complexity, but to show you the range of effects that you can achieve through knitting—and challenge you to learn something new. In so doing, you'll begin to think more like a designer and have the necessary tools to alter existing patterns and create your own designs.

autumn

To me, the knitter's year begins in autumn. Autumn is all about harvesting, saving, and collecting. It's about savoring the light as days get shorter, about soaking up the warmth of Indian summer days, and about preparing for the long gray coldness ahead. It's a time when I come indoors and begin to think about richly colored sweater coats, shawls, hats, wraps, and gloves to stave off the chill. I'm attracted to nature-inspired palettes of wools, alpacas, and cashmeres that beg to be combined in Fair Isle and intarsia designs. My design choices tend to focus on color-work patterns that reflect the deep, saturated colors that blanket the countryside. I'm drawn to classic yarns—heathered alpacas, vegetable-dyed handspun wools, tweeds, marls, and other natural blends—in hues of gold-toned neutrals, vibrant reds and oranges, rich browns, and woodsy greens. I love to collect leaves, pinecones, grasses, seedpods, and dried flowers for texture and color ideas. I like to arrange them in different designs and patterns that inspire my knitting—its color palettes, textures, and shapes.

In *September,* I always find renewed interest in knitting inspired by the spectacular colors of the New England landscape. My design palette is filled with warm tones—amber, coral, gold, pumpkin, sienna, and umber—that my surroundings evoke: a field of hay drying in the late afternoon sun, a simmering pot of squash soup, dried grasses along the roadside.

In *October,* the colors of the harvest are abundant. The leaves are all shades of red, orange, burgundy, chartreuse, bright yellow, then finally brown. Farm stands, fields, and orchards are filled with pumpkins, squash, and apples. Days are crisp, nights are cold, and even the colors of the dying plants in the garden are of interest. October's palette is rich and saturated, centering on all shades of red and orange. The shapes and colors of leaves provide ideas for textured stitches and Fair Isle patterns.

In *November,* the days get shorter and colors fade from the landscape. Everything has gone to seed. Chestnuts and acorns litter the roadside while cattails and tall grasses stand out against blustery blue-gray skies. Golds give way to beiges and browns; reds turn to burgundies and plums; greens dry and fade. Geese fly south across the gray sky creating V-shaped patterns. The palette darkens considerably.

If you take time to appreciate nature's beauty this fall, you'll find your own colorful knitting ideas.

FINISHED SIZE

34½ (41½, 48½, 55½)" (87.5 [105.5, 123, 141] cm) bust circumference (see Notes). Sweater shown measures 41½" (105.5 cm).

YARN

Worsted weight (#4 Medium).

SHOWN HERE: Rowan Silk Tweed (70% silk, 30% cotton; 118 yd [108 m]/50 g): #530 toast (russet), 9 (10, 13, 15) skeins.

NEEDLES

Body and sleeves—size 8 (5 mm): 32" (60 cm) circular (cir). Edging and I-cord—size 7 (4.5 mm): 32" (60 cm) cir and set of 2 double-pointed (dpn). Adjust needle size if necessary to obtain the correct gauge.

NOTIONS

Cable needle (cn); stitch holders; tapestry needle.

GAUGE

16 stitches and 25½ rows = 4" (10 cm) in Grass chart pattern using larger needles; 16 stitches and 23 rows = 4" (10 cm) in Leaf chart pattern using larger needles.

{ designer notes }

Try swatching textures in various yarns to see how the yarn affects the look. I swatched this style in many different types of yarn before I settled on a nub by raw silk. In some yarns and colors, the stitch details all but disappeared. In others, the stitches popped out with crisp definition but the "hand" was too hard. The raw silk I ended up with provided good stitch definition as well as appealing color variation, weight, and drape—perfect!

indian summer
CARDIGAN

Drawn to the textures and colors of the autumn fields, I was inspired by looking closely at the texture of grasses and wheat gone to seed. The perfect little chevrons that seedheads form on alternate sides of a long stem suggested the texture for the high rib of this cardigan. The allover leaf texture is also derived from a simple natural shape.

{ make it your own }

Feel free to choose an entirely different yarn from the one called for in this (or any other project) as long you get the same gauge. Consider the drape of the yarn as well when making substitutions.

stitch guide

DOUBLE INCREASE

Knit the next st through the front loop, then through the back loop, then through the front loop again—3 sts made from 1 st.

NOTES

¤ With the garment laid flat for blocking, the fronts do not meet in the middle and will have about a 1¾" (4.5 cm) gap between them for all sizes. When the garment is tied closed, the fronts meet in the center at the waist to create the effect of waist shaping.

¤ The lower body is worked in one piece to the armholes, then divided for working the fronts and back separately to the shoulders.

LOWER BODY

With larger cir needle, CO 131 (159, 187, 215) sts. Working back and forth in rows, work WS set-up row of Grass chart once; do not rep the set-up row. Rep Rows 1–6 of chart 8 (8, 9, 10) times, then work Rows 7–22 once—65 (65, 71, 77) chart rows total, including set-up row. Work Rows 1–14 of Leaf chart—piece measures about 12¾ (12¾, 13½, 14½)" (32.5 [32.5, 34.5, 37] cm) from CO.

shape neck

NEXT ROW: (RS, Row 15 of chart) P2tog, work in patt to last 2 sts, p2tog—129 (157, 185, 213) sts rem. Work 3 rows even, ending with WS row 18 of chart—piece measures about 13½ (13½, 14¼, 15¼)" (34.5 [34.5, 36, 38.5] cm) from CO.

divide for fronts and back

NEXT ROW: (RS, Row 19 of chart) P2tog, work 28 (35, 42, 49) sts in patt, place 29 (36, 43, 50) sts just worked on holder for right front, work across next 69 (83, 97, 111) sts in patt for back and place them on separate holder, work 28 (35, 42, 49) sts in patt, p2tog—29 (36, 43, 50) sts rem on needle for left front.

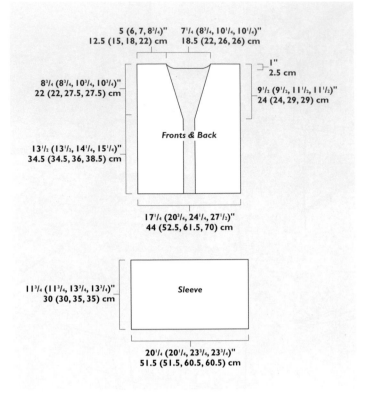

5 (6, 7, 8¾)"
12.5 (15, 18, 22) cm

7¼ (8¾, 10¼, 10¼)"
18.5 (22, 26, 26) cm

1"
2.5 cm

8¾ (8¾, 10¾, 10¾)"
22 (22, 27.5, 27.5) cm

9½ (9½, 11½, 11½)"
24 (24, 29, 29) cm

Fronts & Back

13½ (13½, 14¼, 15¼)"
34.5 (34.5, 36, 38.5) cm

17¼ (20¾, 24¼, 27½)"
44 (52.5, 61.5, 70) cm

11¾ (11¾, 13¾, 13¾)"
30 (30, 35, 35) cm

Sleeve

20¼ (20¼, 23¾, 23¾)"
51.5 (51.5, 60.5, 60.5) cm

Grass

Leaf

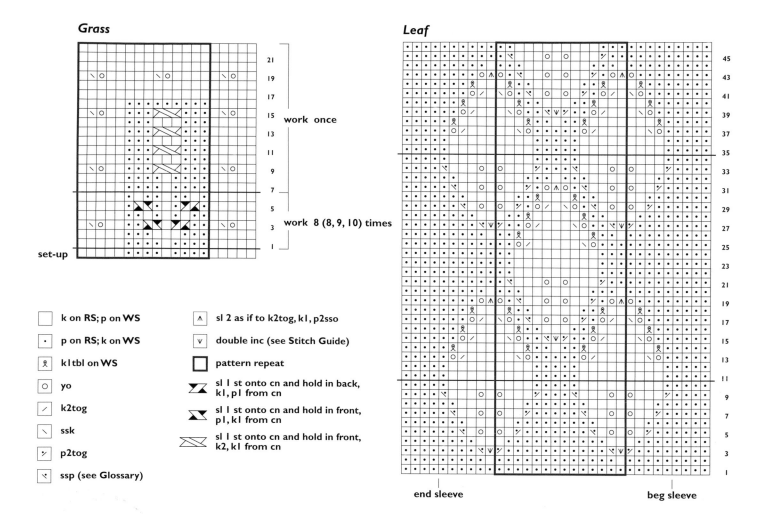

work once

work 8 (8, 9, 10) times

set-up

	k on RS; p on WS
·	p on RS; k on WS
℘	k1tbl on WS
○	yo
╱	k2tog
╲	ssk
⋎	p2tog
⋏	ssp (see Glossary)

∧	sl 2 as if to k2tog, k1, p2sso
v	double inc (see Stitch Guide)
☐	pattern repeat
◥	sl 1 st onto cn and hold in back, k1, p1 from cn
◣	sl 1 st onto cn and hold in front, p1, k1 from cn
✕	sl 1 st onto cn and hold in front, k2, k1 from cn

end sleeve

beg sleeve

13

LEFT FRONT

Working on left front sts only, work 3 rows even in patt, ending with Row 22 of chart. NOTE: Directions for cont neck shaping appear after the foll pattern instructions; read all the way through the next section before proceeding. Cont patt to shoulders by working Rows 23–34 of chart once, then rep Rows 11–34 of chart 1 (1, 2, 2) more time(s), then work Rows 35–46 of chart 1 (1, 0, 0) time—70 (70, 82, 82) Leaf chart rows total. *At the same time*, beg with Row 23 of chart, dec 1 st at neck edge (end of RS rows) every 4 rows 9 (12, 15, 15) times—20 (24, 28, 35) sts rem. When all patt rows have been completed; armhole measures about 8¾ (8¾, 10¾, 10¾)" (22 [22, 27.5, 27.5] cm) from dividing row. BO all sts.

RIGHT FRONT

Return 29 (36, 43, 50) held right front sts to larger cir needle and rejoin yarn with WS facing, ready to work a WS row. Work 3 rows even in patt, ending with Row 22 of chart. NOTE: As for left front, read all the way through the next section before proceeding. Cont in patt to shoulders by working Rows 23–34 of chart once, then rep Rows 11–34 of chart 1 (1, 2, 2) more time(s), then work Rows 35–46 of chart 1 (1, 0, 0) time—70 (70, 82, 82) Leaf chart rows total. *At the same time*, beg with Row 23 of chart, dec 1 st at neck edge (beg of RS rows) every 4 rows 9 (12, 15, 15) times—20 (24, 28, 35) sts rem. When all patt rows have been completed; armhole measures about 8¾ (8¾, 10¾, 10¾)" (22 [22, 27.5, 27.5] cm) from dividing row. BO all sts.

BACK

Return 69 (83, 97, 111) held back sts to larger cir needle and rejoin yarn with WS facing, ready to work a WS row. Work 3 rows even in patt, ending with Row 22 of chart. Work Rows 23–34 of chart once, then rep Rows 11–34 of chart once again.

sizes 34½ (41½)" only

Work Rows 35–40 of chart once—64 (64) Leaf chart rows total completed; armholes measure about 7¾ (7¾)" (19.5 [19.5] cm).

sizes (48½, 55½)" only

Work Rows 11–28 of chart once—(76, 76) Leaf chart rows total completed; armholes measure about (9¾, 9¾)" ([25, 25] cm).

shape neck

NEXT ROW: (RS) Work 26 (30, 34, 41) sts in patt, place center 17 (23, 29, 29) sts on holder, join new yarn, work in patt to end—26 (30, 34, 41) sts rem at each side. Working each side separately, at each neck edge BO 3 sts 2 times—20 (24, 28, 35) sts. Work even in patt until Row 46 (46, 34, 34) has been completed—70 (70, 82, 82) Leaf chart rows total; armholes measure about 8¾ (8¾, 10¾, 10¾)" (22 [22, 27.5, 27.5] cm) from dividing row. BO all sts.

SLEEVES

With larger cir needle, CO 81 (81, 95, 95) sts. Knit 1 WS row. Beg and end where indicated for sleeves, work Rows 1–10 of Leaf chart once, rep Rows 11–34 of chart 2 (2, 3, 3) times, then work Rows 35–46 of chart 1 (1, 0, 0) time—piece measures about 11¾ (11¾, 13¾, 13¾)" (30 [30, 35, 35] cm) from CO. BO all sts.

FINISHING

Block pieces lightly to measurements (see Notes). With yarn threaded on a tapestry needle, sew fronts to back at shoulders. Sew sleeves into armholes, matching center of each sleeve to shoulder seam and easing sleeve evenly to fit. Sew sleeve seams.

neck edging

With smaller cir needle, RS facing, and beg at lower edge of right front, pick up and knit 79 (79, 89, 92) sts along right front edge, 2 sts along shaped right back neck, k17 (23, 29, 29) held back neck sts, pick up and knit 2 sts along shaped left back neck, and 79 (79, 89, 92) sts along left front edge—179 (185, 211, 217) sts total. Knit 2 rows, ending with a RS row. BO all sts on next row knitwise.

belt

With dpn, CO 3 sts. Work 3-st I-cord (see Glossary) until piece measures 78 (85, 92, 99)" (198 [216, 233.5, 251.5] cm) from CO. BO all sts. Beg and end at center front, thread I-cord belt in and out of eyelet holes in Row 19 of Grass chart patt, skipping the center back eyelet.

Lightly steam-block seams as needed. Weave in loose ends.

FINISHED SIZE
34 (40, 46, 52)" (86.5 [101.5, 117, 132] cm) bust circumference, tied with 1¾" (4.5 cm) gap at center front (see Notes). Sweater shown measures 40" (101.5 cm).

YARN
DK weight (#3 Light).

SHOWN HERE: Fiesta Yarns La Luz (100% silk; 220 yd [201 m]/2 oz [56.7 g]): palomino (MC; gold) 7 (8, 9, 10) skeins; vanilla bean (CC; brown), 1 skein for all sizes.

NEEDLES
Size 5 (3.75 mm): straight and 32" (80 cm) circular (cir). Adjust needle size if necessary to obtain the correct gauge.

NOTIONS
Markers (m); stitch holder; 190 (200, 205, 210) size 8/0 matte gold rocaille beads; 380 (390, 400, 410) size 10/0 matte brown beads; tapestry needle; sharp-point sewing needle small enough to pass through smaller beads; sewing thread to match MC for attaching beads.

GAUGE
21 stitches and 31 rows = 4" (10 cm) in stockinette and dot patterns and in body pattern from chart.

{ designer notes }
My original sketch for this style was a very cropped shrug that tied at the front. But thinking that a longer style might be more widely appealing to knitters, I added a "skirt" below the shrug silhouette. The beads help give the cardigan texture, but because they're sewn on after the garment is complete, you can decide whether to include them after you finish knitting.

amber
BEADED CARDIGAN

My goal was to design a cardigan in a shade of gold that captured the look of hay fields drying in the September sun. Apparently, this gold isn't easy to capture with dye on fiber. I found the answer in a handdyed silk yarn with just the right uneven luminosity. I added a sprinkling of gold matte beads to mimic the texture of field seeds—wheat grains, grass, and corn kernels.

{ make it your own }
If you like the cropped shrug in the original sketch (shown above), simply omit the bottom half of the sweater. To prevent the lower edge from rolling, begin by working a small lace border.

stitch guide

DOT PATTERN
(WORKED IN MULTIPLES OF 4 STS + 3)

ROWS 1, 5, AND 7: (RS) Knit.

ROWS 2, 4, AND 6: (WS) Purl.

ROW 3: K1, *p1, k3; rep from * to last 2 sts, p1, k1.

ROW 8: Rep Row 2.

Repeat Rows 1–8 for pattern.

NOTES

¤ This garment is styled so the fronts do not meet in the center. Tie the fronts with a smaller or larger space between them to customize the fit and accommodate slightly smaller, larger, or in-between sizes.

¤ If during shaping there are not enough stitches to work a decrease with its companion yarnover, work the stitches in stockinette instead to maintain the correct stitch count.

BACK

With CC and straight needles, CO 105 (121, 137, 153) sts. Knit 1 RS row. Change to MC and purl 1 WS row. SET-UP ROW: (RS) K1 (selvedge st; work in St st throughout), work Row 1 of Edging chart over center 103 (119, 135, 151) sts, k1 (selvedge st; work in St st throughout). Cont in patt, work Rows 2–10 of chart—piece measures about 1½" (3.2 cm) from CO. NEXT ROW: (RS) K1 (selvedge st), k2tog, work Row 1 of Body chart over center 99 (115, 131, 147) sts, ssk, k1 (selvedge st)—103 (119, 135, 151) sts rem. Working sts at each side in St st, work Rows 2–10 once, then dec 1 st at each end of needle as before on Row 11—101 (117, 133, 149) sts rem. Cont in patt, dec 1 st at each end of needle every 10 rows 8 more times (see Notes)—85 (101, 117, 133) sts rem. Work even in patt until 12-row rep has been worked at total of 8 times, then work Rows 1–5 once more—101 chart rows total; piece measures about 14½" (37 cm) from CO for all sizes. Knit 1 WS row for garter ridge. NEXT ROW: (RS) K1 (selvedge st), work Row 1 of dot patt (see Stitch Guide) over center 83 (99, 115, 131) sts, k1 (selvedge st). Cont in patt, inc 1 st at each end of needle on Row 3 of patt, work 7 rows even, then inc 1

st at each end of needle on foll RS row (Row 3 of patt), working new sts into patt—89 (105, 121, 137) sts. Work even in patt until piece measures 17 (17½, 18, 18½)" (43 [44.5, 45.5, 47] cm) from CO, ending with a WS row.

shape armholes

Cont in patt, BO 3 (4, 5, 6) sts at beg of next 2 rows, then BO 2 (3, 4, 5) sts at beg of foll 2 rows, then BO 2 (2, 3, 4) sts at beg of foll 2 rows—75 (87, 97, 107) sts rem. DEC ROW: (RS) K2, k2tog, work in patt to last 4 sts, ssk, k2—2 sts dec'd. Dec 1 st each end of needle in this manner on the next 1 (2, 3, 4) RS row(s)—71 (81, 89, 97) sts rem. Cont even until armholes measure 7 (7½, 8, 8½)" (18 [19, 20.5, 21.5] cm), ending with a WS row.

shape neck and shoulders

Cont in patt, work 29 (33, 36, 39) sts, place center 13 (15, 17, 19) sts on holder, join new yarn, work in patt to end—29 (33, 36, 39) sts at each side. Working each side separately, at each neck edge BO 4 (5, 5, 5) sts once, then BO 4 sts once, then BO 3 sts once—18 (21, 24, 27) sts at each side; armholes measure about 8 (8½, 9, 9½)" (20.5 [21.5, 23, 24] cm). NOTE: Neck shaping continues while shoulder shaping is introduced; read all the way through the next section before proceeding. Cont to shape neck by dec 1 st at each neck edge 2 times and *at the same time,* at each armhole edge BO 5 (6, 7, 8) sts 2 times, then BO 6 (7, 8, 9) sts once—no sts rem.

RIGHT FRONT

With CC and straight needles, CO 49 (57, 65, 73) sts. Knit 1 RS row. Change to MC and purl 1 WS row. SET-UP ROW: (RS) K1 (selvedge st; work in St st throughout), work Row 1 of Edging chart over center 47 (55, 63, 71) sts, k1 (selvedge st; work in St st throughout). Cont in patt, work Rows 2–10 of chart—piece measures about 1½" (3.2 cm) from CO. NEXT ROW: (RS) K1 (selvedge st), k2tog, work Row 1 of Body chart over center 43 (51, 59, 67) sts, ssk, k1 (selvedge st)—47 (55, 63, 71) sts rem. Working sts at each side in St st, work Rows 2–10. NEXT ROW: (RS; Row 11 of chart) Work in patt to last 3 sts, ssk, k1—46 (54, 62, 70) sts rem. Cont in patt, dec 1 st at side edge (end of RS rows) every 10 rows 8 more times—38 (46, 54, 62) sts rem. Work even in patt until 12-row rep has been worked a total of 8 times, then work Rows 1–5 once more—101 chart rows total; piece measures about 14½" (37 cm) from CO for all sizes. Knit 1 WS row for garter ridge. NEXT ROW: (RS) K1 (selvedge st), k1, work Row 1 of dot patt over next 35 (43, 51, 59) sts, k1 (selvedge st). Cont in patt, inc 1 st at end of needle on Row 3 of patt, work 7 rows even, then inc 1 st at end of needle on foll RS row (Row 3 of patt), working new sts into patt—40 (48, 56, 64) sts; with RS facing, there are 1 selvedge st, 1 knit st, 35 (43, 51, 59) sts in patt, 2 sts for partial patt rep, 1 selvedge st. Work even in patt until piece measures 16½ (17, 17½, 18)" (42 [43, 44.5, 45.5] cm) from CO, ending with a WS row.

		k on RS; p on WS
•		p on RS; k on WS
o		yo
/		k2tog

\		ssk
⋏		sl 2 sts as if to k2tog, k1, p2sso
▓		no stitch
▢		pattern repeat

Edging

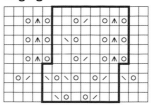

Body

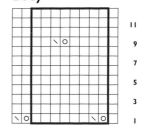

Front Trim

Cuff

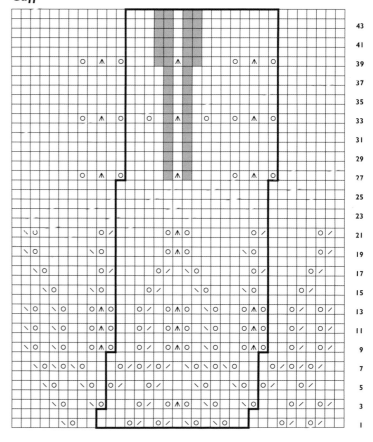

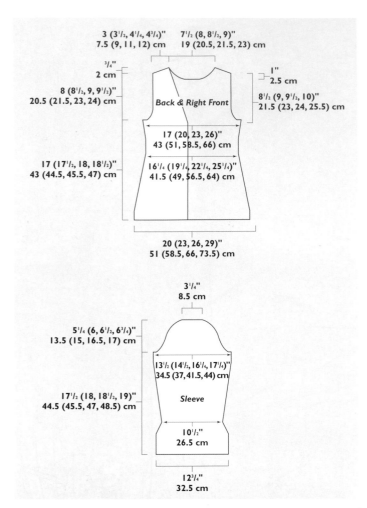

3 (3½, 4¼, 4¾)"
7.5 (9, 11, 12) cm

7½ (8, 8½, 9)"
19 (20.5, 21.5, 23) cm

¾"
2 cm

1"
2.5 cm

8 (8½, 9, 9½)"
20.5 (21.5, 23, 24) cm

Back & Right Front

8½ (9, 9½, 10)"
21.5 (23, 24, 25.5) cm

17 (20, 23, 26)"
43 (51, 58.5, 66) cm

17 (17½, 18, 18½)"
43 (44.5, 45.5, 47) cm

16¼ (19¼, 22¼, 25¼)"
41.5 (49, 56.5, 64) cm

20 (23, 26, 29)"
51 (58.5, 66, 73.5) cm

3¼"
8.5 cm

5¼ (6, 6½, 6¾)"
13.5 (15, 16.5, 17) cm

13½ (14½, 16¼, 17¼)"
34.5 (37, 41.5, 44) cm

17½ (18, 18½, 19)"
44.5 (45.5, 47, 48.5) cm

Sleeve

10½"
26.5 cm

12¾"
32.5 cm

shape neck and armhole

DEC ROW: (RS) K2, ssk, work in patt to end of row—39 (47, 55, 63) sts rem. Work 2 rows even in patt, ending with a RS row— piece measures 17 (17½, 18, 18½)" (43 [44.5, 45.5, 47] cm) from CO. NOTE: Armhole shaping is introduced while neck shaping continues; read all the way through the next section before proceeding. Keeping in patt, dec 1 st at neck edge (beg of RS rows) every 4th row 14 (16, 17, 18) more times—15 (17, 18, 19) sts total removed at neck edge. *At the same time,* at armhole edge (beg of WS rows) BO 3 (4, 5, 6) sts once, then BO 2 (3, 4, 5) sts once, then BO 2 (2, 3, 4) once, then dec 1 at armhole edge (end of RS rows) 2 (3, 4, 5) times by working in patt to last 4 sts, ssk, k2—9 (12, 16, 20) sts total removed at armhole edge; 16 (19, 22, 25) sts rem when all neck and armhole shaping has been completed. Work even until armhole measures 8 (8½, 9, 91½)" (20.5 [21.5, 23, 24] cm), ending with a RS row.

shape shoulder

BO 5 (6, 7, 8) sts at beg of next 2 WS rows, then BO rem 6 (7, 8, 9) sts at beg of foll WS row—no sts rem.

LEFT FRONT

With CC and straight needles, CO 49 (57, 65, 73) sts. Knit 1 RS row. Change to MC and purl 1 WS row. SET-UP ROW: (RS) K1 (selvedge st; work in St st throughout), work Row 1 of Edging chart over center 47 (55, 63, 71) sts, k1 (selvedge st; work in St st throughout). Cont in patt, work Rows 2–10 of chart—piece measures about 1½" (3.2 cm) from CO. NEXT ROW: (RS) K1 (selvedge st), k2tog, work Row 1 of Body chart over center 43 (51, 59, 67) sts, ssk, k1 (selvedge st)—47 (55, 63, 71) sts rem. Working sts at each side in St st, work Rows 2–10. NEXT ROW: (RS; Row 11 of chart) K1, k2tog, work in patt to end—46 (54, 62, 70) sts rem. Cont in patt, dec 1 st at side edge (beg of RS rows) every 10 rows 8 more times—38 (46, 54, 62) sts rem. Work even in patt until 12-row rep has been worked a total of 8 times, then work Rows 1–5 once more—101 chart rows total; piece measures about 14½" (37 cm) from CO for all sizes. Knit 1 WS row for garter ridge. NEXT ROW: (RS) K1 (selvedge st), work Row 1 of dot patt over next 35 (43, 51, 59) sts, k1, k1 (selvedge st). Cont in patt, inc 1 st at beg of needle on Row 3 of patt, work 7 rows even, then inc 1 st at end of needle on foll RS row (Row 3 of patt), working new sts into patt—40 (48, 56, 64) sts; with RS facing, there are 1 selvedge st, 2 sts in partial patt rep, 35 (43, 51, 59) sts in patt, 1 knit st, 1 selvedge st. Work even in patt until piece measures 16½ (17, 17½, 18)" (42 [43, 44.5, 45.5] cm) from CO, ending with a WS row.

shape neck and armhole

DEC ROW: (RS) Work in patt to last 3 sts, k2tog, k2—39 (47, 55, 63) sts rem. Work 3 rows even in patt, ending with a WS row—piece measures 17 (17½, 18, 18½)" (43 [44.5, 45.5, 47] cm) from CO. NOTE: Armhole shaping is introduced while neck shaping continues; read all the way through the next section before proceeding. Keeping in patt, dec 1 st at neck edge (end of RS rows) every 4th row 14 (16, 17, 18) more times—15 (17, 18, 19) sts total removed at neck edge. *At the same time,* at armhole edge (beg of RS rows) BO 3 (4, 5, 6) sts once, then BO 2 (3, 4, 5) sts once, then BO 2 (2, 3, 4) once, then dec 1 at armhole edge (beg of RS rows) 2 (3, 4, 5) times by working first 4 sts as k2, k2tog—9 (12, 16, 20) sts total removed at armhole edge; 16 (19, 22, 25) sts rem when all neck and armhole shaping has been completed. Work even until armhole measures 8 (8½, 9, 9½)" (20.5 [21.5, 23, 24] cm), ending with a WS row.

shape shoulder

BO 5 (6, 7, 8) sts at beg of next 2 RS rows, then BO rem 6 (7, 8, 9) sts at beg of foll RS row—no sts rem.

SLEEVES (MAKE 2)

With CC and straight needles, CO 67 sts for all sizes. Knit 1 RS row. Change to MC and purl 1 WS row. Work Rows 1–44 of Cuff chart, dec as shown on Rows 27 and 39—55 sts rem; piece measures about 5½" (14 cm) from CO. Change to dot patt beg with Row 3, and inc 1 st at each end of needle on Row 3, then every 12 (8, 6, 6) rows 7 (10, 14, 17) more times, working new sts into patt—71 (77, 85, 91) sts. Cont even in patt until piece measures 17½ (18, 18½, 19)" (44.5 [45.5, 47, 48.5] cm) from CO, ending with a WS row.

shape cap

Cont in patt, BO 3 (4, 5, 6) sts at beg of next 2 rows, then BO 2 (3, 4, 5) sts at beg of foll 2 rows, then BO 2 (2, 3, 4) sts at beg of foll 2 rows—57 (59, 61, 61) sts rem. DEC ROW: (RS) K2, k2tog, work in patt to last 4 sts, ssk, k2—2 sts dec'd. Dec 1 st each end of needle in this manner every other RS row 0 (0, 2, 0) more times, then every 6 rows 4 (5, 4, 6) times—47 sts rem for all sizes. BO 2 sts at beg of next 4 rows, then BO 3 sts at beg of foll 4 rows, then BO 5 sts at beg of foll 2 rows—17 sts rem. BO all sts.

FINISHING

Lightly steam-block pieces to measurements. With MC threaded on a tapestry needle, sew fronts to back at shoulders. Sew sleeves into armholes, then sew sleeve and side seams. Lightly steam seams, if necessary.

front trim

With MC, cir needle, RS facing, and beg at CO edge of right front, pick up and knit 65 (67, 69, 71) sts along right front to beg of neck shaping, 33 (34, 35, 36) sts along right front neck, 17 sts along shaped right back neck, k13 (15, 17, 19) held back neck sts, pick up and knit 17 sts along shaped left back neck, 33 (34, 35, 36) sts along left front neck to beg of neck shaping, and 65 (67, 69, 71) sts along left front—243 (251, 259, 267) sts total. Knit 1 WS row. Work Rows 1–10 of Front Trim chart. BO all sts.

ties (make 2)

With MC and straight needles, CO 1 st.

ROW 1: (RS) (K1, p1, k1) all in same st—3 sts.

ROWS 2, 4, AND 6: K1, purl to last st, k1.

ROW 3: [K1, M1 (see Glossary)] 2 times, k1—5 sts.

ROW 5: K2, M1, k1, M1, k2—7 sts.

ROW 7: K2, M1, k3, M1, k2—9 sts.

ROW 8: [K1, p3] 2 times, k1.

ROWS 9 AND 11: Knit.

ROW 10: K1, p7, k1.

Rep Rows 8–11 until piece measures 8" (20.5 cm) from CO, ending with a WS row. BO all sts, leaving a long tail for attaching tie. With tail threaded on a tapestry needle, use the invisible horizontal seam (see Glossary) to sew the BO edge of tie to RS of front trim pick-up row, centered on the garter ridge between the body and dot patts, so that tie is on top of front trim. Make and attach a second tie the same as the first.

beads

Using sharp-point sewing needle, anchor a double strand of sewing thread to RS of front trim pick-up row at lower edge of right front (see Glossary for stitching instructions). *[Thread 1 gold and 2 brown beads, lay beads flat and close together following pick-up row of front trim, work a small running stitch through the fabric] 4 times, make a small backstitch to secure the last 12 beads; rep from * up the right front, around the back neck, and back down to the left front. Fasten off thread securely.

design *workshop* #1

FINDING INSPIRATION

EVERY DESIGN BEGINS WITH A SPARK of inspiration. For me, inspiration can come from just about anywhere. You, too, can find inspiration in your everyday surroundings. All you have to do is train your eye to look closely at the world around you and to think in terms of individual design elements. You'll soon find ideas everywhere you look.

Most of my ideas come from nature, fashion, history, and art. I love to collect natural objects, pieces of vintage textiles, and loads of books, to which I frequently refer for ideas. I collect paint chips from hardware stores. I peruse interior design, gardening, and other magazines and tear out images whenever something catches my eye. Whenever I can, I look in vintage clothing stores, antique shops, galleries, and museums. I take walks in the woods and along the beach. I do all of this to gain inspiration. Whenever something strikes my fancy, I make a quick sketch and scrawl some notes to help me remember what it was.

I begin my knitwear design process by pulling together a pile of the stuff I've gathered—found objects, pages from magazines, sketches, scraps of fabric or handmade paper, postcards, autumn leaves, antique lace—anything and everything that appeals to me at the moment. I sort through the pile to find commonalities of color, texture, or structure. I arrange the items in a collage that tells a "story" or creates a particular mood. I then step back and think of ways I can translate that story or mood into knitwear.

For this workshop, you'll create your own mood board. It has nothing to do with knitting in particular, but playing with a handful of things to reveal a common theme is a fun and easy way to exercise your creativity.

GATHER IDEAS

To begin, flip through magazines, keeping an eye out for patterns, colors, and shapes that are pleasing to you. Check out fashion magazines for modern silhouettes and gardening magazines for unusual color combinations. Look at home decorating magazines for fabric and rug designs and textures. Peruse architecture magazines for interesting forms. You get the idea. Tear out anything that holds your attention for more than a few seconds. It doesn't need to be a sweater—it just needs to have an interesting color, texture, or pattern.

Go outside and take a really close look at nature. Stroll along a beach and collect shells, rocks, sea glass, and driftwood. Take a walk in a forest, field, or garden and pay attention to the leaves, flowers, moss, and bark. Spend some time at art galleries, museums, antique shops, and clothing stores. Take note of whatever catches your eye. Perhaps you are drawn to the clean modern lines of Danish furniture, the rich colors of Tibetan rugs, or the delicate lace on a Victorian gown. Make a little sketch of whatever it is so you'll remember when you get back home. And wherever you live, visit the Internet. You can draw inspiration from the vast desert southwest as easily as from the crowded streets of New York City.

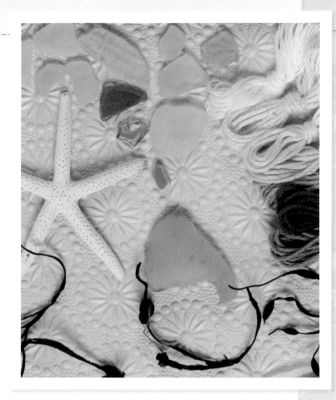

COMMON THEMES

Next, sort what you've collected into groupings that represent common themes. A dragonfly's wing, a leaf skeleton, and a scrap of vintage lace from a yard sale may seem unrelated, but gathered together, they tell a story about laciness. Look for stories in your collections and fasten the items that tell a story to a piece of foam-core to make your own mood board. I created the mood board shown here around objects I found on the beach—sea glass, shells, and rocks—with attention to the textures of sea urchins, starfish, and sand dollars that my children collected. This collection evokes the casual feeling of lazy summer days. Your board will tell the story you've discovered.

Congratulations! You've mastered the first step in designing!

FINISHED SIZE

36 (40½, 45)" (91.5 [103, 114.5] cm) bust circumference, buttoned. Sweater shown measures 40½" (103 cm).

YARN

Chunky weight (#5 Bulky).

SHOWN HERE: Manos del Uruguay Wool (100% wool; 135 yd [123 m]/100 g): #M Bing cherry (MC; dark burgundy), 3 (3, 4) skeins; #32 gasoline (grayed lavender), 1 (1, 2) skein(s); #54 red, #V cinnamon (dark orange), #37 thrush (golden brown), #28 copper (light orange), #42 marl (medium tan), #65 wheat (gold), #55 dark olive, #67 light loden, #68 citric (lime), #D spruce (blue-green), #30 silica (light beige), #41 thistle (purple), and #08 black, 1 skein each.

NOTE: The manufacturer suggests working the yarn shown at a worsted-weight (#4 Medium) gauge, but for this project it has been deliberately worked more loosely at a chunky (#5 Bulky) gauge.

NEEDLES

Size 9 (5.5 mm). Adjust needle size if necessary to obtain the correct gauge.

NOTIONS

Tapestry needle; size F/5 (3.75 mm) crochet hook; seven ½" (1.3 cm) buttons with shanks.

GAUGE

14 stitches and 20½ rows = 4" (10 cm) in stockinette color-work patterns from charts.

{ designer notes }

This type of intarsia represents the ultimate challenge in knitting. But the stunning finished piece that lies at the end of the process makes it all worthwhile. Think of it like a jigsaw puzzle—it takes a bit of work for the image to appear.

walk in the woods
JACKET

Near my house is a small mountain where I like to collect leaves and wildflowers. After a recent excursion, I laid a collection of colorful leaves, flowers, and grasses on my scanner and scanned them against different colored papers and fabrics. When I put the leaves against a burgundy background, I knew I had the right combination for a cozy autumn jacket!

¤ Work Rows 1–10 of the charts using the Fair Isle or stranded color-work method, carrying the unused color loosely across the back of the work. For the remaining chart rows, use the stockinette intarsia method with separate strands of yarn for each section, crossing the yarns at each color change to prevent leaving holes.

BACK

With MC and using the long-tail method (see Glossary), CO 69 (77, 85) sts. Beg and ending with a RS row, knit 3 rows. Change to medium tan. Knit 1 WS row, then work 2 rows in St st, ending with a WS row—piece measures about 1" (2.5 cm) from CO. Establish patt from Row 1 of Back chart (page 28), beg and end where indicated for your size. Work Rows 2–52 in patt from charts (see Note), dec 1 st each end of needle on Rows 3, 11, 17, 23, 27, 31, 35, and 39 as shown—53 (61, 69) sts rem; piece measures about 11¼" (28.5 cm) from CO. Beg on Row 53, inc 1 st each end of needle on Rows 53, 57, 61, 65, and 69 as shown—63 (71, 79) sts rem. Work even until Row 76 (78, 82) has been completed—piece measures about 15¾ (16¼, 17)" (40 [41.5, 43] cm) from CO.

shape armholes

Beg on Row 77 (79, 83) of chart, BO 2 (3, 4) sts at beg of next 2 rows, then BO 2 sts at beg of foll 2 rows—55 (61, 67) sts rem. Dec 1 st each end of needle every other row 2 (3, 4) times, then every 4th row 1 (2, 2) time(s)—49 (51, 55) sts rem. Work even until Row 116 (120, 126) has been completed.

shape neck and shoulders

On Row 117 (121, 127), work 17 (18, 19) sts in patt, join new yarn and BO center 15 (15, 17) sts, work in patt to end—17 (18, 19) sts at each side. Working each side separately, at each neck edge BO 2 sts once, then BO 1 st once. *At the same time,* beg on Row 119 (123, 129) when armholes measure about 8½ (9, 9½)" (21.5 [23, 24] cm), at each armhole edge BO 5 sts 2 times, then BO 4 (5, 6) sts once—no sts rem.

{ make it your own }

You have to go to a special place in your knitting psyche for this type of challenging project. But I do have some tips to help you along.

· Don't balk at making butterflies or bobbins for the various color blocks. Before beginning this project, make about eight "reelings" of each color by wrapping yarn around four fingers about a dozen times, then wrapping each bundle around the middle and cutting and pulling the yarn end through to tighten it. Store the reelings in Ziploc bags. That way, you're sure to have some of every color with you—without lugging entire balls of yarn.

· You will have a lot (dozens or hundreds) of ends to weave in. Take a Zen approach and accept that you'll have to devote at least four hours to weaving in ends. In the greater scheme of things, it's really not all that long.

· This yarn felts nicely, so consider using the leftover for a sturdy striped tote.

RIGHT FRONT

With MC and using the long-tail method, CO 35 (39, 43) sts. Beg and ending with a RS row, knit 3 rows. Change to medium tan. Knit 1 WS row, then work 2 rows in St st, ending with a WS row—piece measures about 1" (2.5 cm) from CO. Work Rows 1–52 of Right Front chart (page 29) ending where indicated for your size, and dec 1 st at end of Rows 3, 11, 17, 23, 27, 31, 35, and 39 as shown—27 (31, 35) sts rem; piece measures about 11¼" (28.5 cm) from CO. Beg on Row 53, inc 1 st at end of Rows 53, 57, 61, 65, and 69 as shown—32 (36, 40) sts.

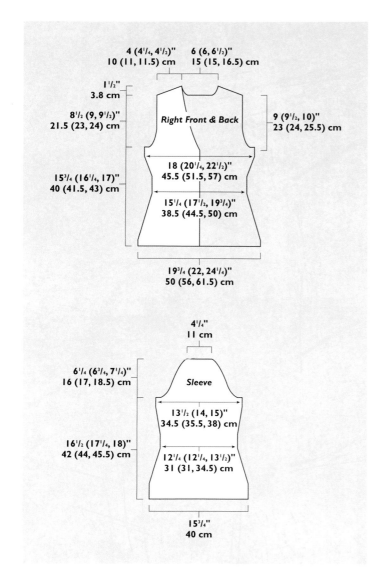

4 (4¼, 4½)"
10 (11, 11.5) cm

6 (6, 6½)"
15 (15, 16.5) cm

1½"
3.8 cm

8½ (9, 9½)"
21.5 (23, 24) cm

Right Front & Back

9 (9½, 10)"
23 (24, 25.5) cm

15¾ (16¼, 17)"
40 (41.5, 43) cm

18 (20¼, 22½)"
45.5 (51.5, 57) cm

15¼ (17½, 19¾)"
38.5 (44.5, 50) cm

19¾ (22, 24¼)"
50 (56, 61.5) cm

4¼"
11 cm

6¼ (6¾, 7¼)"
16 (17, 18.5) cm

Sleeve

13½ (14, 15)"
34.5 (35.5, 38) cm

16½ (17¼, 18)"
42 (44, 45.5) cm

12¼ (12¼, 13½)"
31 (31, 34.5) cm

15¾"
40 cm

shape neck and armhole

NOTE: Neck and armhole shaping shown on chart are worked at the same time; read all the way through the next section before proceeding. Work even in patt until Row 74 (76, 80) of chart has been completed. Beg on Row 75 (77, 81) of chart, dec 1 st at neck edge (beg of RS rows) every other row 3 times, then every 4th row 8 (8, 9) times—11 (11, 12) sts total removed at neck edge. *At the same time,* when piece mea-

sures about 15¾ (16¼, 17)" (40 [41.5, 43] cm) from CO, shape armhole beg on Row 78 (80, 84) by BO 2 (3, 4) sts at beg of next WS row, then BO 2 sts at beg of foll WS row, then dec 1 st at armhole edge (end of RS rows) every other row 2 (3, 4) times, then every 4th row 1 (2, 2) time(s)—7 (10, 12) sts total removed at armhole edge; 14 (15, 16) sts rem when all neck and shoulder shaping has been completed. Work even in patt until Row 119 (123, 129) has been completed.

shape shoulder

Beg on Row 120 (124, 130), BO 5 sts 2 times, then BO 4 (5, 6) sts once—no sts rem.

LEFT FRONT

With MC and using the long-tail method, CO 35 (39, 43) sts. Beg and ending with a RS row, knit 3 rows. Change to medium tan. Knit 1 WS row, then work 2 rows in St st, ending with a WS row—piece measures about 1" (2.5 cm) from CO. Work Rows 1–52 of Left Front chart beg where indicated for your size, and dec 1 st at beg of Rows 3, 11, 17, 23, 27, 31, 35, and 39 as shown—27 (31, 35) sts rem; piece measures about 11¼" (28.5 cm) from CO. Beg on Row 53, inc 1 st at beg of Rows 53, 57, 61, 65, and 69 as shown—32 (36, 40) sts.

shape neck and armhole

NOTE: As for right front, neck and armhole shaping are worked at the same time; read all the way through the next section before proceeding. Work even in patt until Row 74 (76, 80) of chart has been completed. Beg on Row 75 (77, 81), dec 1 st at neck edge (end of RS rows) every other row 3 times, then every 4th row 8 (8, 9) times—11 (11, 12) sts total removed at neck edge. *At the same time,* when piece measures about 15¾ (16¼, 17)" (40 [41.5, 43] cm) from CO, shape armhole beg on Row 77 (79, 83) by BO 2 (3, 4) sts at beg of next RS row, then BO 2 sts at beg of foll RS row, then dec 1 st at armhole edge (beg of RS rows) every other row 2 (3, 4) times, then every 4th row 1 (2, 2) time(s)—7 (10, 12) sts total removed at armhole edge; 14 (15, 16) sts rem when all neck and shoulder shaping have been completed. Work even in patt until Row 118 (122, 128) has been completed.

shape shoulder

Beg on Row 119 (123, 129), BO 5 sts 2 times, then BO 4 (5, 6) sts once—no sts rem.

dark burgundy (MC)

red

dark orange

golden brown

light orange

medium tan

gold

dark olive

light loden

lime

blue-green

light beige

grayed lavender

purple

black

Back

131

121

111

101

91

81

71

61

51

41

31

21

11

1

end · end · end
45" 40½" 36"

↑
center st

beg · beg · beg
36" 40½" 45"

Right Front

131

121

111

101

91

81

71

61

51

41

31

21

11

1

end end end
45" 40½" 36"

Left Front

131

121

111

101

91

81

71

61

51

41

31

21

11

1

beg beg beg
36" 40½" 45"

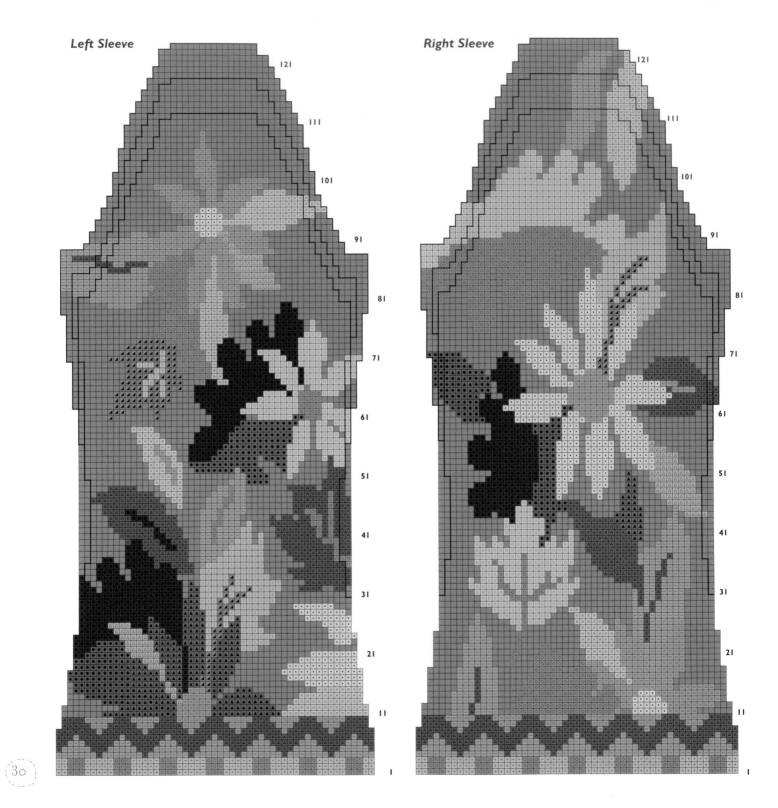

Left Sleeve

Right Sleeve

121

111

101

91

81

71

61

51

41

31

21

11

1

LEFT SLEEVE

With MC and using the long-tail method, CO 55 sts. Beg and ending with a RS row, knit 3 rows. Change to medium tan. Knit 1 WS row, then work 2 rows in St st, ending with a WS row—piece measures about 1" (2.5 cm) from CO. Work Rows 1–50 of Left Sleeve chart, dec 1 st each end of Rows 9, 13, 19, and 25 for all sizes, then on Rows 31 and 37 for sizes 36" and 40½" only as shown— 43 (43, 47) sts rem; piece measures about 10¾" (27.5 cm) from CO.

size 36" only

Cont in patt, inc 1 st each end of needle on Rows 51 and 71 as shown—47 sts.

size 40½" only

Cont in patt, inc 1 st each end of needle on Rows 51, 63, and 75 as shown—49 sts.

size 45" only

Cont in patt, inc 1 st each end of needle on Rows 63, 71, and 79 as shown—53 sts.

all sizes

Work even until Row 80 (84, 88) has been completed—piece measures about 16½ (17¼, 18)" (42 [44, 45.5] cm) from CO.

shape cap

Beg on Row 81 (85, 89), BO 2 (3, 4) sts at beg of next 2 rows—43 (43, 45) sts rem. Dec 1 st each end of needle every other row 5 (4, 5) times, then every 4th row 2 (3, 3) times—29 sts rem for all sizes. Dec 1 st each end of needle every other row 5 times, then BO 2 sts at beg of next 2 rows, ending with Row 112 (118, 124)—15 sts rem. BO rem sts.

RIGHT SLEEVE

Work as for left sleeve, substituting right sleeve chart.

FINISHING

Block pieces to measurements. With MC threaded on a tapestry needle, sew fronts to back at shoulders.

edging

With waste yarn, mark positions for 7 button loops on right front, the lowest 8" (20.5 cm) up from CO edge, the highest even with beg of neck shaping, and the rem 5 evenly spaced in between. With MC, crochet hook, RS facing, and beg at CO edge of right front, work a row of single crochet (sc; see Glossary for crochet instructions) along right front opening, across back neck, and down left front opening to end at CO edge of left front. Change to dark orange. With RS still facing, and work a row of rev sc along left front, back neck, and right front to highest marked button loop position, *ch 5, close loop by working a slip stitch in base of ch, work rev sc to next marked position; rep from * 5 more times, ch 5, close loop with slip stitch in base of chain, work in rev sc to lower edge of right front. Fasten off last st.

seams

With MC threaded on a tapestry needle, sew sleeve caps into armholes. Sew sleeve and side seams. Weave in loose ends. Lightly wet-block seams with iron and damp cloth as needed. Sew buttons to left front, opposite button loops.

31

FINISHED SIZE

About 35¼ (40¼, 46¾)" (89.5 [102, 118.5] cm) bust circumference, buttoned with ¾" (2 cm) front edgings overlapped. Jacket shown measures 40¼" (102 cm).

YARN

Chunky weight (#5 Bulky).

SHOWN HERE: Reynolds Andean Alpaca Regal (90% alpaca, 10% wool; 110 yd [100 m]/100 g): #104 dark chocolate (A), 11 (12, 13) balls; #606 coral (B), #24 brick (C), #26 copper (D), #5225 fuchsia (E), #713 golden straw (G), #980 leaf (H, light green), #8 brass (I; olive), and #422 celadon (J; teal), 2 balls each; #25 dark mauve (F), 1 ball.

NEEDLES

Body and sleeves—size 9 (5.5 mm). Collar—size 7 (4.5 mm): 32" (60 cm) circular (cir). Adjust needle size if necessary to obtain the correct gauge.

NOTIONS

Markers (m); cable needle (cn); stitch holders; tapestry needle; five 1⅜" (3.5 cm) toggle buttons; size H/8 (4.75 mm) crochet hook.

GAUGE

15½ stitches and 19 rows = 4" (10 cm) in stockinette stitch on larger needles; 3-stitch front edging measures ¾" (2 cm) wide in seed stitch on larger needles.

{ designer notes }

To freshen the intarsia floral motif from the boxy tunics popular during the late 1980s, I used an updated silhouette. I wrapped the roses around the border in a long, belted sweater-coat. To keep things interesting, I added a bit of stitch texture.

coral roses
JACKET

I can't resist roses. Because the Maine winters are too harsh for me to grow my own, I admire them at the market—buckets of luscious little rose bouquets in deep pinks, corals, and burnt yellow shades. Inspired by these colors, I knitted an intarsia swatch of heirloom roses in coral and pink, then translated it into a feminine jacket.

{ make it your own }

If an entire jacket is too much floral intarsia for you, omit the color work and knit the jacket in a solid color or use the single rose motif on a tote bag or pillow. For a fancy edging, pick up stitches around the edges and work the multicolor motif from the sleeve cuff as a ruffle.

SEED STITCH (WORKED OVER 3 STS)
ALL ROWS: K1, p1, k1.

NOTE

¤ Work Rows 7 and 8 of the body charts using the Fair Isle or stranded color-work method, carrying the unused color loosely across the back of the work. For all other color work, use the stockinette intarsia method with separate strands of yarn for each section, crossing the yarns around each other at each color change to prevent leaving holes.

BACK

With A and larger needles, CO 79 (89, 101) sts. Beg and ending with a WS row, knit 2 rows then purl 1 row. EYELET ROW: (RS) K2 (4, 4), *yo, ssk, k2; rep from * to last st, k1. Purl 1 WS row. Beg and ending where indicated for your size, work Rows 1–26 of Back and Sleeves chart (see Note). Cont in patt from chart, dec 1 st each end of needle on Rows 27, 33, 39, 43, 47, 51, 55, 59, and 63 as foll: (RS) K1, k2tog, work in patt to last 4 sts, ssk, k1—61 (71, 83) sts rem after Row 63. Cont in patt until Row 66 of chart has been completed—piece measures about 14¾" (37.5 cm) from CO. Cont with A in St st, dec 1 st each end of needle on next RS row—59 (69, 81) sts. Work 7 rows even in St st, ending with as WS row—piece measures about 16½" (42 cm) from CO. INC ROW: (RS) K1, M1 (see Glossary), knit to last st, M1, k1—2 sts inc'd. Work 5 rows even. Cont in St st, rep the shaping of the last 6 rows 2 more times, then work inc row once more—67 (77, 89) sts. Work even until piece measures 20½ (21, 21½)" (52 [53.5, 54.5] cm) from CO, ending with a WS row. Establish placement of Center Back chart on next row as foll: (RS) K20 (25, 31) with A, place marker (pm), work Row 1 of Center Back chart over next 30 sts, pm, k17 (22, 28) with A. NOTE: The number of sts on each side of the center back chart is deliberately different in order for the rose to appear centered on the back of the jacket. Working sts on each side of chart with A, work even in patt until piece measures 21 (21½, 22)" (53.5 [54.5, 56] cm) from CO, ending with a WS row.

shape armholes

Cont working marked sts as charted, BO 3 (3, 4) sts at beg of next 2 rows, then BO 2 (2, 3) sts at beg of foll 2 rows, then dec 1 st each end of needle as for waist shaping on the next 1 (3, 5) RS row(s)—55 (61, 65) sts rem. Work even in patt until Row 38 of chart has been completed, then cont in St st with A until armholes measure 8½ (9, 9½)" (21.5 [23, 24] cm), ending with a WS row.

Back and Sleeves

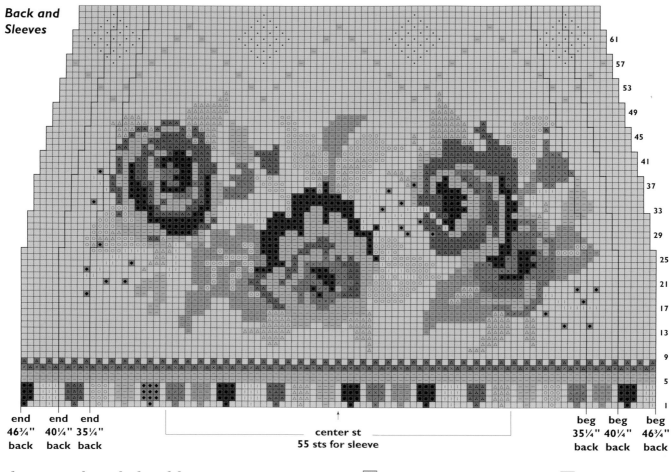

																															61
																															57
																															53
																															49
																															45
																															41
																															37
																															33
																															29
																															25
																															21
																															17
																															13
																															9
																															5
																															1

end 46¾" back   end 40¼" back   end 35¼" back

center st 55 sts for sleeve

beg 35¼" back   beg 40¼" back   beg 46¾" back

shape neck and shoulders

K20 (22, 23), join new ball of yarn and BO center 15 (17, 19) sts, knit to end—20 (22, 23) sts each side. Working each side separately, at each neck edge BO 3 sts once, then BO 2 sts once and *at the same time*, at each armhole edge, BO 5 (5, 6) sts once then BO 5 (6, 6) sts 2 times—no sts rem.

LEFT FRONT

With A and larger needles, CO 43 (48, 54) sts. Knit 1 WS row. NEXT ROW: (RS) Knit to last 3 sts, work 3 front edge sts in seed st (see Stitch Guide). NEXT ROW: (WS) Work 3 seed sts, purl to end. EYELET ROW: (RS) K3 (4, 2), *yo, ssk, k2; rep from * to last 4 sts, k1, work 3 seed sts. NEXT ROW: (WS) Work 3 seed sts, purl to end. Maintaining 3 front edge sts in seed st as established and beg where indicated for your size, work Rows 1–26 of Left Front chart over 40 (45, 51) sts.

▢ dark chocolate; k on **RS**, p on **WS**		◆ dark mauve
· dark chocolate; p on **RS**, k on **WS**		○ golden straw
— coral			leaf
◉ brick		= brass
⁂ copper		△ celadon
✕ fuchsia		

Left Front

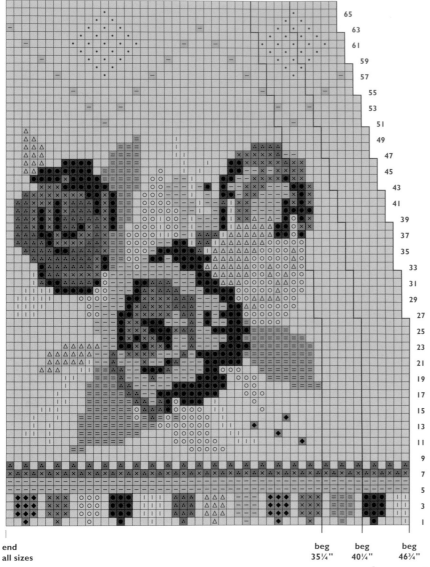

Center Back

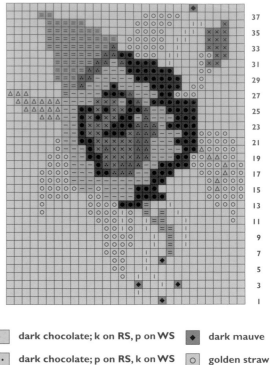

	dark chocolate; k on RS, p on WS		dark mauve
•	dark chocolate; p on RS, k on WS	○	golden straw
−	coral		leaf
	brick	=	brass
	copper	△	celadon
×	fuchsia		

Cont in patt from chart, dec 1 st at beg of needle on Rows 27, 33, 39, 43, 47, 51, 55, 59, and 63 as foll: (RS) K1, k2tog, work in patt to last 3 sts, work 3 seed sts—34 (39, 45) sts rem after Row 63. Cont in patt until Row 66 of chart has been completed—piece measures about 14¾" (37.5 cm) from CO. Maintaining 3 front edge sts in seed st and working rem sts in St st with A, dec 1 st at beg of needle on next RS row—33 (38, 44) sts rem. Work 7 rows even in St st, ending with a WS row—piece measures about 16½" (42 cm) from CO.

shape side, neck, and armhole

NOTE: Neck shaping is introduced while side shaping is still in progress; read the next sections all the way through before proceeding. INC ROW: (RS) K1, M1, knit to last 3 sts, work 3 seed sts—1 st inc'd. Work 5 rows even. Cont in St st, rep the shaping of the last 6 rows 2 more times, then work inc row once more—4 sts total added at side edge (beg of RS rows), including first inc row. *At the same time*, when piece mea-

Right Front

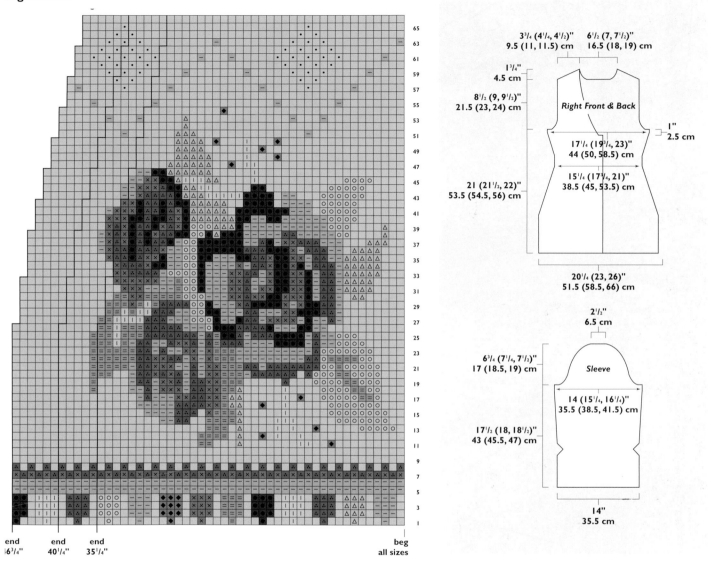

sures 20 (20½, 21)" (51 [52, 53.5] cm) from CO, beg neck shaping on the next WS row as foll: BO 3 front edge sts, purl to end. NOTE: Armhole shaping is introduced after side shaping is finished, but while neck shaping is still in progress; read the next sections all the way through before proceeding. At neck edge (end of RS rows), dec 1 st every RS row 7 (8, 9) times, then every other RS row 6 times as foll: Work in patt to last 4 sts including any required side or armhole

shaping, ssk, k2—16 (17, 18) sts total removed from neck edge, including 3 BO edge sts. *At the same time,* when piece measures 21 (21½, 22)" (53.5 [54.5, 56] cm) from CO, shape armhole by BO 3 (3, 4) sts at beg of next RS row, then BO 2 (2, 3) sts at beg of foll RS row, then dec 1 st at beg of needle as for waist shaping on next 1 (3, 5) RS row(s)—6 (8, 12) sts total removed from armhole edge; 15 (17, 18) sts rem when all shaping has been completed. Cont even until armhole measures 8½ (9, 9½)" (21.5 [23, 24] cm), ending with a WS row.

shape shoulder

BO 5 (5, 6) sts at beg of next RS row, then BO 5 (6, 6) sts at beg of foll 2 RS rows—no sts rem.

RIGHT FRONT

With waste yarn, mark positions of 5 buttons on left front edging, the lowest about 9½ (10, 10½)" (24 [25.5, 26.5] cm) up from CO edge, the highest ½" (1.3 cm) below beg of neck shaping, and the rem 3 evenly spaced in between. Compare right and left fronts frequently as you work, and whenever the right front reaches the same length as a marked button position on the left front make a buttonhole on the next RS row by working first 3 sts of row as k1, yo, k2tog. With A and larger needles, CO 43 (48, 54) sts. Knit 1 WS row. NEXT ROW: (RS) Work 3 front edge sts in seed st, knit to end. NEXT ROW: (WS) Purl to last 3 sts, work 3 seed sts. EYELET ROW: (RS) Work 3 seed sts, k1, *k2, ssk, yo; rep from * to last 3 (4, 2) sts, k3 (4, 2). NEXT ROW: (WS) Purl to last 3 sts, work 3 seed sts. Maintaining 3 front edge sts in seed st as established and working buttonholes as required, work Rows 1–26 of Right Front chart over 40 (45, 51) sts, ending where indicated for your size. Cont in patt from chart, dec 1 st at end of needle on Rows 27, 33, 39, 43, 47, 51, 55, 59, and 63 as foll: (RS) Work 3 seed sts, work in patt to last 3 sts, ssk, k1—34 (39, 45) sts rem after Row 63. Cont in patt until Row 66 of chart has been completed—piece measures about 14¾" (37.5 cm) from CO. Maintaining 3 front edge sts in seed st and working rem sts in St st with A, dec 1 st at end of needle on next RS row—33 (38, 44) sts rem. Work 7 rows even in St st, ending with as WS row—piece measures about 16½" (42 cm) from CO.

shape side, neck, and armhole

NOTE: As for left front, neck shaping begins while side shaping is still in progress and continues after armhole shaping is introduced; read the next sections all the way through before proceeding. INC ROW: (RS) Work 3 seed sts, knit to last st, M1, k1—1 st inc'd. Work 5 rows even. Cont in St st, rep the shaping of the last 6 rows 2 more times, then work inc row once more—4 sts total added at side edge (end of RS rows), including first inc row. *At the same time*, when piece measures 20 (20½, 21)" (51 [52, 53.5] cm) from CO, beg neck shaping on the next RS row as foll: BO 3 front edge sts, knit to end. At neck edge (beg of RS rows), dec 1 st every RS row 7 (8, 9) times, then every other RS row 6 times as

foll: K2, k2tog, work to end including any required side or armhole shaping—16 (17, 18) sts total removed from neck edge, including 3 BO edge sts. *At the same time*, when piece measures 21 (21½, 22)" (53.5 [54.5, 56] cm) from CO, shape armhole by BO 3 (3, 4) sts at beg of next WS row, then BO 2 (2, 3) sts at beg of foll WS row, then dec 1 st at end of needle as for waist shaping on next 1 (3, 5) RS row(s)—6 (8, 12) sts total removed from armhole edge; 15 (17, 18) sts rem when all shaping has been completed. Cont even until armhole measures 8½ (9, 9½)" (21.5 [23, 24] cm), ending with a RS row.

shape shoulder

BO 5 (5, 6) sts at beg of next WS row, then BO 5 (6, 6) sts at beg of foll 2 WS rows—no sts rem.

SLEEVES (MAKE 2)

With A and larger needles, CO 55 sts for all sizes. Beg and ending with a WS row, knit 2 rows then purl 1 row. EYELET ROW: (RS) K2, *yo, ssk, k2; rep from * to last st, k1. Purl 1 WS row. Beg and ending where indicated for sleeve, work Rows 1–8 of Back and Sleeves chart. NEXT ROW: (RS) With A, p5, *k5, p5; rep from * to end. NOTE: There will be deliberate "blips" of color on the RS where sts in color C were purled with A. Work sts as they appear (knit the knits and purl the purls) until piece measures 5½" (14 cm) from CO, ending with a WS row. NEXT ROW: (RS) P5, [sl 5 sts onto cn and hold in back, p5, k5 from cn] 5 times. NEXT ROW: (WS) *P5, k5; rep from * to last 5 sts, k5. Work sts as they appear until piece measures 7½" (19 cm) from CO, ending with a WS row.

size 35¼" only

Change to St st and work even until piece measures 17½" (44.5 cm) from CO, ending with a WS row.

sizes (40¼, 46¾)" only

INC ROW: (RS) K1, M1, knit to last st, M1, k1—2 sts inc'd. Cont in St st, inc 1 st each end of needle in this manner every (40, 14) rows (1, 3) more time(s)—(59, 63) sts. Work even in St st until piece measures (18, 18½)" ([45.5, 47] cm) from CO, ending with a WS row.

shape cap

BO 3 (3, 4) sts at beg of next 2 rows, then BO 2 (2, 3) sts at beg of foll 2 rows, then dec 1 st each end of needle as for waist shaping on the next 4 RS rows—37 (41, 41) sts rem. Dec 1 st each end of needle every 4 rows 1 (2, 3) time(s)—35 (37, 35) sts rem. Dec 1 st each end of needle every RS row 5 (4, 3) times—25 (29, 29) sts rem. BO 2 sts at beg of next 2 rows, then BO 3 (4, 4) sts at beg of foll 4 rows—9 sts rem. BO all sts.

FINISHING

Lightly steam-block all pieces to measurements. With A threaded on a tapestry needle, sew fronts to back at shoulders.

collar

With A, smaller cir needle, WS facing, and beg at start of left front neck shaping, pick up and knit 58 (60, 62) sts along left front neck to shoulder seam, 31 (33, 35) sts across back neck, and 58 (60, 62) sts along right front neck to end at start of right front neck shaping—147 (153, 159) sts total. NOTE: Picking up from the WS will cause the pick-up line to show on the RS of the jacket, but it will be concealed when collar is folded back.

SET-UP ROW: (WS of collar, RS of jacket) *P3, k3; rep from * to last 3 sts, p3.

The shawl collar is shaped using short-rows (see Glossary) without wrapping any sts to produce a deliberate effect of small holes at the turning points. Cont as foll:

SHORT-ROW 1: (RS of collar; WS of jacket) Work in rib patt to last 3 sts, turn.

SHORT-ROW 2: (WS of collar; RS of jacket) Work in rib patt to last 3 sts, turn.

SHORT-ROW 3: Work in rib patt to 3 sts before last turning point, turn.

SHORT-ROWS 4–28: Rep Short-row 3—14 turning points at each end of collar after completing Short-row 28; 63 (69, 75) sts at center between last pair of turning points.

NEXT ROW: (RS of collar) Work in rib patt to end of row. Work across all sts in rib patt for 3 rows, ending with a WS collar row—collar measures about 6" (15 cm) from pick-up row at center back neck. BO all sts.

With A threaded on a tapestry needle, sew sleeve caps into armholes. Sew side and sleeve seams. Sew short selvedges at each end of collar to BO sts at start of neck shaping.

belt and belt loops

With A and larger needles, CO 11 sts. SET-UP ROW: (RS) *K1, p1; rep from * to last st, k1. Cont in established rib until piece measures about 59 (64, 71)" (150 [162.5, 180.5] cm) from CO. BO all sts.

With A and crochet hook, make two crochet chains (see Glossary) each 2" (5 cm) long, leaving long tails for attaching belt loops. Sew one belt loop to each side seam with the loop centered on the straight section worked even at the waist.

Weave in loose ends. Sew buttons to left front edging, opposite buttonholes. Thread belt through belt loops and tie in front.

FINISHED SIZE

CAPELET: 48" (122 cm) circumference at lower edge, 16" (40.5 cm) circumference at neck, and 20" (51 cm) long from lower edge to top of collar.

GAUNTLETS: 12" (30.5 cm) circumference at lower edge, 8" (20.5 cm) circumference at hand above thumb opening, and 14" (35.5 cm) long overall.

YARN

Worsted weight (#4 Medium).

SHOWN HERE: Tahki Stacy Charles Donegal Tweed (100% wool; 183 yd [167 m]/100 g): #892 apple green, #863 red, #848 oatmeal, #846 maize, #869 brown, #874 burgundy, #895 charcoal, #839 olive, and #8933 pumpkin, 1 skein each for capelet and gauntlet set.

NEEDLES

Capelet—size 8 (5 mm): 32" and 16" (60 and 40 cm) circular (cir). Gauntlets—size 9 (5.5 mm) set of 5 double-pointed (dpn). Adjust needle size if necessary to obtain the correct gauge.

NOTIONS

Markers (m); tapestry needle; small stitch holders for gauntlets.

GAUGE

18 stitches and 25 rounds = 4" (10 cm) in pattern from capelet chart worked in the round; 16 stitches and 24 rounds = 4" (10 cm) in pattern from gauntlets chart worked in the round.

fair isle capelet
AND GAUNTLETS

For this design, I wanted to capture the classic styling of the traditional Shetland Fair Isle yoke sweater in the heathered, natural shades of the late autumn landscape. I blew up the scale of a typical Shetland sweater, deconstructed it to just the patterned yoke, and translated it into a tweedy, marled yarn in the vegetable-dyed colors of dried fields and fallen leaves. Then I made a pair of unfinished sleeves, or gauntlets, to wear with it.

stitch guide

BOBBLE

Knit into the front, back, and front of next st—3 sts made from 1 st. Turn, p3, turn, sl 1 as if to knit with yarn in back, k2tog, pass slipped st over—3 sts dec'd back to 1 st.

CAPELET

With apple green and longer cir needle, CO 216 sts. Place marker (pm) and join for working in rnds, being careful not to twist sts. Work 3 rnds in k3, p3 rib as foll: *K3, p3; rep from * to end. Knit 3 rnds, purl 1 rnd, then knit 2 rnds—piece measures about 1¼" (3.2 cm) from CO. Establish patt from Rnd 1 of Capelet chart by working 12-st rep 18 times around. Work Rnds 2–100 of chart, dec 1 st at beg of each rep on Rnds 61, 66, 71, 78, 83, 88, 96, and 100 as shown on chart, and changing to shorter cir needle when there are too few sts to fit around longer needle—72 sts rem after completing Rnd 100; piece measures about 17¼" (44 cm) from CO.

collar

With burgundy, work 16 rnds in k2, p2 rib as foll: *K2, p2; rep from * to end. Knit 2 rnds—collar measures about 2¾" (7 cm) from end of chart. BO all sts loosely with burgundy.

FINISHING

Weave in loose ends. Block lightly to measurements.

GAUNTLETS

NOTE: For one of the sample gauntlets, Rnds 56 and 57 are worked with red instead of burgundy as shown on chart.

right hand

With red, CO 48 sts. Arrange sts evenly on 4 dpn, place marker (pm), and join for working in rnds, being careful not to twist sts. Purl 1 rnd. Establish patt from Rnd 1 of Gauntlet chart by working 6-st rep 8 times around. Work Rnds 2–65 of chart, dec 2 sts in each rep on Rnd 46 as shown on chart—32 sts rem; piece measures about 10¾" (27.5 cm) from CO. Mark position of thumb on next rnd as foll: (Rnd 66 of chart)

{ make it your own }

For shorter fingerless mitts, cast on and work 1 rnd as for gauntlets. Work Rnds 1–3 of Gauntlet chart, skip Rnds 4–39, then work Rnds 40–84 for a total length of about 8" (20.5 cm). Bind off mitt and work thumb as for gauntlets.

Cont in patt, work 20 sts, sl next 5 sts onto holder, use the backward-loop method (see Glossary) to CO 5 sts over gap, work 7 sts in patt to end. Work Rnds 67–84 of chart—piece measures about 14" (35.5 cm) from CO. With maize, BO all sts knitwise.

thumb

Place 5 held thumb sts on dpn and join oatmeal to beg of sts with RS facing. K5 held sts, pick up and knit 3 sts from side of thumb opening, 5 sts from base of sts CO at top of thumb, and 3 sts from other side of thumb opening—16 sts total. Arrange sts as evenly as possible on 3 dpn, pm, and join for working in the rnd. Knit 5 rnds, then [purl 1 rnd, knit 1 rnd] 2 times. With oatmeal, BO all sts knitwise.

left hand

CO and work as for right hand until Rnd 65 of chart has been completed—32 sts rem; piece measures about 10¾" (27.5 cm) from CO. Mark position of thumb on next rnd as foll: (Rnd 66 of chart) Cont in patt, work 7 sts, sl next 5 sts onto holder, use the backward-loop method to CO 5 sts over gap, work 20 sts in patt to end. Complete as for right hand. Work thumb as for right hand.

FINISHING

Weave in loose ends. Block lightly as needed.

Capelet

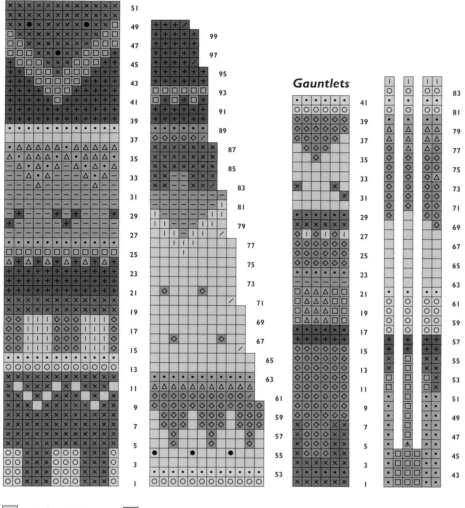

Gauntlets

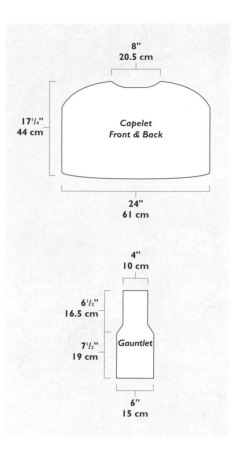

○	apple green	
✕	red	
	oatmeal	
I	maize	
◇	brown	
+	burgundy	
□	charcoal	

—	olive
△	pumpkin
•	purl with color shown
╱	k2tog with color shown
ʌ	sl 2 as if to k2tog, k1, pass 2 slipped sts over
●	bobble with color shown (see Stitch Guide)

winter

Winter is the perfect time of year for knitting. Quiet indoor time encourages us to unwind to the rhythm of clicking needles. The world outside slows to a calmer, more serene pace inspired by the landscape outside, I turn to more subdued colors as well. My designs revolve around mostly solid-colored textures—cable patterns inspired by the grays, creams, whites, beiges, blues, and browns that reflect the various textures of barren trees, fields covered in drifted snow, cloudy skies, and the tiny patterns in snowflakes and ice crystals. Sometimes simple and sometimes complex, the patterns of winter often emphasize softness and warmth and focus on natural fibers that imbue a sense of coziness.

Although *December* ought to be a time to relax and celebrate the end of the year with family and friends, we often overextend ourselves in the harried rush to attend parties, buy presents, and mail cards. In December, the days are very short and evening darkness begins in early afternoon. But we can choose to light that darkness and bring to it a quiet, festive warmth. In the town where I live, we place candles in our windows, wrap trees with tiny lights, and build fires on our hearths that sparkle against the dark. Winter is when I like to add a bit—not too much—of shimmer to my designs to give them an elegant air of holiday cheer.

January brings peace and solitude after the holiday rush. Outside, the world is all about texture and pattern. Snow blankets the ground and the ripples and waves of the drifts suggest loose cables. Against the gray skyline, the silhouettes of intertwined bare tree branches inspire a complex cabled coat. The comfort of a cup of freshly brewed coffee inspires a chunky, latte-colored oversize tunic. A pointelle pattern on the tunic's sleeves is reminiscent of fir trees against a bare ground.

In *February*, the air is frigid and the sky is often a crisp clear blue. The world is crusted over with ice and snow. A palette of browns and blues prevails. The miniscule flowers of frost on windowpanes reveal intricate patterns, sun glistening on ice crystals suggests a touch of beading, and icicles hanging from the eaves resemble an irregular lace border. Shadows on the snow create a palette of cool blues and whites in undulating stripes.

On a quiet winter day, look outside your window and see what textures you can find in snowdrifts, evergreens, and ice-coated branches.

FINISHED SIZE

37 (41, 48, 51)" (94 [104, 122, 129.5] cm) bust circumference. Shrug shown measures 41" (104 cm).

YARN

Worsted weight (#4 Medium) or one strand each of DK weight (#3 Light) and fingering weight (#1 Super Fine) held together.

SHOWN HERE: Rowan Lurex Shimmer (80% viscose, 20% polyester; 103 yd [94 m]/25 g): #331 claret, 7 (8, 8, 9) balls. NOTE: This yarn has been discontinued; you may substitute Lang/Berroco Lurex in color #0060 burgundy or Katia/Knitting Fever Gatsby in color #16 burgundy.

Rowan Kidsilk Haze (70% super kid mohair, 30% silk; 229 yd [209 m]/25 g): #595 liqueur (wine), 3 (4, 4, 5) balls.

NEEDLES

Body and sleeves—size 10½ (6.5 mm). Edging—size 8 (5 mm). Adjust needle size if necessary to obtain the correct gauge.

NOTIONS

Stitch holders; one 1½" (3.8 cm) brooch or decorative pin closure; tapestry needle.

GAUGE

22 stitches (2 pattern repeats wide) and 32 rows (4 pattern repeats high) = 5¼" (13.5 cm) wide and 5½" (14 cm) high in pattern from Body chart on larger needles. NOTE: If combining two yarns as for the shrug shown, the gauge is with one strand of each yarn held together.

{ designer notes }

No one has a lot of extra time around the holidays, but because this cropped piece is worked with two strands of yarn on larger needles, it knits up quickly. I deliberately designed it to hang open for a casual look or to fasten with a piece of jewelry to dress it up.

shimmer lace
SHRUG

In this lace shrug, I wanted a bit of shimmer for a festive feeling. I knew that the sparkle would impart a dressy look, but I wanted a garment that could be worn at other times as well. I found the answer by working a thin Lurex yarn that reflects the light along with a fine mohair that softens the shimmer.

{ make it your own }

For a less dressy look, substitute a solid yarn (such as Tahki Dream) for the sparkly Lurex. Instead of a brooch closure, attach single crochet ties at the neck or substitute coordinating sheer silk or satin ribbon ties. For shorter sleeves, work fewer rows before beginning with the cap shaping.

¤ Use one strand of each yarn held together throughout.

¤ If during shaping there are not enough stitches to work a decrease with its companion yarnover, work the stitches in stockinette instead to avoid throwing off the stitch count. For example, the back for sizes 37" and 48" does not have enough stitches between the beginning and ending points to work both the decreases next to the pattern repeat box and their corresponding yarnovers that appear at the edges of the chart. So for these two sizes, work the first and last pattern stitches as k1 instead.

¤ The sleeve cuff is worked from side to side, then stitches are picked up along the straight selvedge of the cuff and worked upwards for the main part of the sleeve.

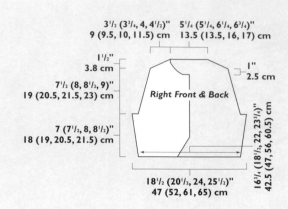

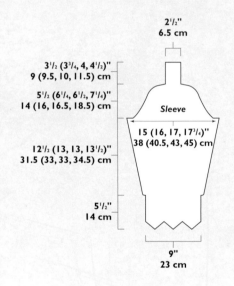

BACK

With larger needles, one strand of each yarn held tog, and using the long-tail method (see Glossary), CO 70 (78, 92, 100) sts. Knit 1 WS row. SET-UP ROW: (RS) K1 (selvedge st; work in St st), work Row 1 of Body chart (page 50) over center 68 (76, 90, 98) sts beg and ending where indicated for your size, k1 (selvedge st; work in St st). NOTE: Do not work any dec or yo without its companion yo or dec (see Notes). Work 7 rows even in patt, ending with WS Row 8 of chart. Inc 1 st each end of needle inside selvedge sts every time you work Row 1 of chart, rep Rows 1–8 of chart 4 more times, working new sts into patt (see Notes)—78 (86, 100, 108) sts; 40 chart rows completed; piece measures about 7" (18 cm) from CO. Work in patt for 0 (½, 1, 1½)" (0 [1.3, 2.5, 3.8] cm) more, ending with a WS row—piece measures 7 (7½, 8, 8½)" (18 [19, 20.5, 21.5] cm) from CO.

shape armholes

BO 4 (4, 5, 5) sts at beg of next 2 rows, then BO 3 (3, 4, 4) sts at beg of foll 2 rows, then BO 2 (2, 3, 3) sts at beg of foll 2 rows—60 (68, 76, 84) sts rem. Dec 1 st each end of needle every 4 rows 4 (7, 8, 9) times—52 (54, 60, 66) sts rem. Cont even until armholes measure 7½ (8, 8½, 9)" (19 [20.5, 21.5, 23] cm), ending with a WS row.

shape shoulders

BO 4 (4, 4, 5) sts at beg of next 6 rows, then BO 3 (4, 5, 4) sts at beg of next 2 rows—22 (22, 26, 28) sts rem. Place sts on holder for back neck.

piece measures about 7" (18 cm) from CO. Work in patt for 0 (½, 1, 1½)" (0 [1.3, 2.5, 3.8] cm) more, ending with a RS row—piece measures 7 (7½, 8, 8½)" (18 [19, 20.5, 21.5] cm) from CO.

shape armhole

BO 4 (4, 5, 5) sts at beg of next WS row, then BO 3 (3, 4, 4) sts at beg of foll WS row, then BO 2 (2, 3, 3) sts at beg of foll WS row—30 (34, 38, 42) sts rem. Dec 1 st at armhole edge (end of RS rows) every 4 rows 4 (7, 8, 9) times—26 (27, 30, 33) sts rem. Work even in patt until armhole measures 6½ (7, 7½, 8)" (16.5 [18, 19, 20.5] cm), ending with a WS row.

shape neck

At neck edge (beg of RS rows), BO 5 (5, 6, 6) sts once, then BO 3 (3, 4, 4) sts once, then BO 2 (2, 2, 3) sts once, ending with a WS row—16 (17, 18, 20) sts rem; armhole measures about 7½ (8, 8½, 9)" (19 [20.5, 21.5, 23] cm).

shape shoulder

BO 1 more st at neck edge at beg of next RS row and *at the same time* shape shoulder by BO 4 (4, 4, 5) sts at beg of next 3 WS rows, then BO 3 (4, 5, 4) sts at beg foll WS row—no sts rem.

LEFT FRONT

With larger needles, one strand of each yarn held tog, and using the long-tail method, CO 26 (30, 37, 41) sts. Knit 1 WS row. SET-UP ROW: (RS) K1 (selvedge st; work in St st), work Row 1 of Body chart over center 24 (28, 35, 39) sts beg and ending where indicated for your size, k1 (selvedge st; work in St st). NOTE: As for back and right front, do not work any dec or yo without its companion yo or dec. Cont in patt, shape front and side edges as foll: Inc 1 st at front edge (end of RS rows) Inside selvedge st every RS row 9 times and *at the same time* inc 1 st at side edge (beg of RS rows) inside selvedge st the next 4 times you work Row 1 of chart, working new sts into patt—39 (43, 50, 54) sts. Work even until Rows 1–8 have been worked a total of 5 times—40 chart rows completed; piece measures about 7" (18 cm) from CO. Work in patt for 0 (½, 1, 1½)" (0 [1.3, 2.5, 3.8] cm) more, ending with a WS row—piece measures 7 (7½, 8, 8½)" (18 [19, 20.5, 21.5] cm) from CO.

RIGHT FRONT

With larger needles, one strand of each yarn held tog, and using the long-tail method, CO 26 (30, 37, 41) sts. Knit 1 WS row. SET-UP ROW: (RS) K1 (selvedge st; work in St st), work Row 1 of Body chart over center 24 (28, 35, 39) sts beg and ending where indicated for your size, k1 (selvedge st; work in St st). NOTE: As for back, do not work any dec or yo without its companion yo or dec. Cont in patt, shape front and side edges as foll: Inc 1 st at front edge (beg of RS rows) inside selvedge st every RS row 9 times and *at the same time* inc 1 st at side edge (end of RS rows) inside selvedge st the next 4 times you work Row 1 of chart, working new sts into patt—39 (43, 50, 54) sts. Work even until Rows 1–8 have been worked a total of 5 times—40 chart rows completed;

k on RS; p on WS

· p on RS; k on WS

o yo on both RS and WS

/ k2tog on RS

⅄ k2tog on WS

\ ssk on RS

⅄ k3tog on RS; p3tog on WS

ᴧ sl 1, p2tog, psso on WS

pattern repeat

Cuff

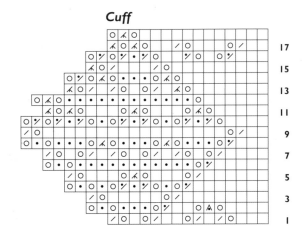

17
15
13
11
9
7
5
3
1

Body

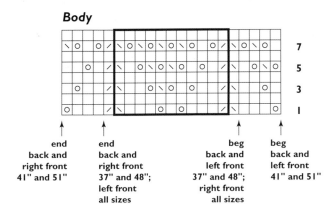

7
5
3
1

end
back and
right front
41" and 51"

end
back and
right front
37" and 48";
left front
all sizes

beg
back and
left front
37" and 48";
right front
all sizes

beg
back and
left front
41" and 51"

shape armhole

BO 4 (4, 5, 5) sts at beg of next RS row, then BO 3 (3, 4, 4) sts at beg of foll RS row, then BO 2 (2, 3, 3) sts at beg of foll RS row—30 (34, 38, 42) sts rem. Dec 1 st at armhole edge (beg of RS rows) every 4 rows 4 (7, 8, 9) times—26 (27, 30, 33) sts rem. Work even in patt until armhole measures 6½ (7, 7½, 8)" (16.5 [18, 19, 20.5] cm), ending with a RS row.

shape neck

At neck edge (beg of WS rows), BO 5 (5, 6, 6) sts once, then BO 3 (3, 4, 4) sts once, then BO 2 (2, 2, 3) sts once, ending with a RS row—16 (17, 18, 20) sts rem; armhole measures about 7½ (8, 8½, 9)" (19 [20.5, 21.5, 23] cm).

shape shoulder

BO 1 more st at neck edge at beg of next WS row and *at the same time* shape shoulder by BO 4 (4, 4, 5) sts at beg of next 3 RS rows, then BO 3 (4, 5, 4) sts at beg foll RS row—no sts rem.

SLEEVES (MAKE 2)

With larger needles, one strand of each yarn held tog, and using the long-tail method, CO 15 sts. Rep Rows 1–18 of Cuff chart 3 times—54 chart rows completed; piece measures about 9" (23 cm) from CO. BO all sts. Hold cuff with RS facing so straight selvedge at beg of RS cuff rows runs horizontally across the top of the piece and join both yarns to upper right-hand corner. With larger needles and one strand of each yarn held tog, pick up and knit 57 sts evenly spaced along straight edge of cuff. Purl 1 WS row. SET-UP ROW: (RS) K1 (selvedge st; work in St st), work 11-st patt rep marked by red box on Body chart 5 times, k1 (selvedge st; work in St st). Cont in patt, beg on the next RS row inc 1 st each end of needle inside selvedge sts every 20 (12, 8, 8) rows 3 (5, 7, 9) times, working new sts into patt—63 (67, 71, 75) sts. Cont even until piece measures 12½ (13, 13, 13½)" (31.5 [33, 33, 34.5] cm) from pick-up row and about 18 (18½, 18½, 19)" (45.5 [47, 47, 48.5] cm) from deepest point of cuff, ending with a WS row.

shape cap

BO 4 (4, 5, 5) sts at beg of next 2 rows, then BO 3 (3, 4, 4) sts at beg of foll 2 rows, then BO 2 (2, 3, 3) sts at beg of foll 2 rows—45 (49, 47, 51) sts rem. Dec 1 st each end of needle every 4 rows 4 (4, 6, 6) times, then every 2 rows 3 (5, 2, 4) times—31 sts rem for all sizes. BO 5 sts at beg of next 4 rows—11 sts rem; sleeve cap measures about 5½ (6¼, 6½, 7¼)" (14 [16, 16.5, 18.5] cm). Cont even in patt until saddle shoulder extension measures 3½ (3¾, 4, 4½)" (9 [9.5, 10, 11.5] cm) above last BO row. Place sts on holder.

FINISHING

Lightly steam-block pieces to measurements. With yarn threaded on a tapestry needle (or mohair yarn only if using yarn combination as shown), sew selvedges of sleeve extensions to fronts and back at shoulders. Sew sleeve caps into armholes. Sew side seams. Sew each sleeve seam from pick-up row above cuff to armhole, leaving sides of cuff open.

neck edging

With larger needles, one strand of each yarn held tog, RS facing, and beg at right front neck edge, pick up and knit 24 (24, 28, 31) sts along right front neck edge to saddle shoulder seam, k11 held right sleeve sts, k22 (22, 26, 28) held back neck sts, k11 held left sleeve sts, pick up and knit 24 (24, 28, 31) sts along left front neck edge—92 (92, 104, 112) sts total. NEXT ROW: (WS) *K1, p1; rep from *. BO all sts in established rib patt on next row.

Weave in loose ends.

FINISHED SIZE

37½ (43¼, 48½)" (95 [110, 123] cm) bust circumference. Sweater shown measures 43¼" (110 cm).

YARN

Chunky weight (#5 Bulky).

SHOWN HERE: Reynolds Andean Alpaca Regal (90% alpaca, 10% wool; 110 yd [100 m]/100 g): #6 natural, 8 (9, 10) balls.

NEEDLES

Size 10 (6 mm). Adjust needle size if necessary to obtain the correct gauge.

NOTIONS

Markers (m); cable needle (cn); tapestry needle; sharp-point sewing needle and matching thread for inserting zipper; 13 (14, 15)" (33 [35.5, 38] cm) matching separating sport zipper.

GAUGE

14½ stitches and 20 rows = 4" (10 cm) in stockinette stitch; 21 stitches and 20 rows = 4" (10 cm) in cable pattern from chart, after dropping sts as indicated and with fabric relaxed.

{ designer notes }

I didn't want to fuss with a lot of shaping on the collar, so I just knitted a large rectangle. For the cuffs, I knitted another rectangle of the cable pattern, turned it sideways, and picked up stitches from the edge for the rest of the sleeve. Minimal shaping on the stockinette-stitch body helps keep the knitting straightforward.

snowdrift
CARDIGAN

I like the way that the wind can blow the snow into heavy drifts. I decided that a cable pattern would be just right to echo this texture in a soft and enveloping garment. I chose a big flowing cable that results from intentionally dropped stitches. The pattern is surprisingly easy to knit and the effect is soft and wavy with a nice drape—just like the snow!

{ make it your own }

The key to success with this design is to drop the appropriate stitches as you work the bind-off row. If these stitches aren't dropped, the cuffs and collar will be too tight, way too small, and the soft, undulating cable pattern won't show up.

DROP STITCH

Drop the indicated st from the needle and allow it to ravel down to its starting yo, gently coaxing the st as necessary so it ladders evenly, then immediately make a yo to replace the dropped st and maintain the correct st count.

NOTES

¤ The shoulder seams for this garment are offset toward the back and the back armholes are shorter than the front armholes. Sloped shoulder shaping is worked only on the back; the front shoulders are bound off straight across.

¤ When sewing in the sleeves, lay the garment flat to find the top of the armhole opening (about 1" [2.5 cm] forward of the shoulder seam) and match the center of the sleeve cap to the top of the armhole, not to the shoulder seam.

BACK

CO 67 (77, 87) sts. NEXT ROW: (WS) K2, *p3, k2; rep from * to end. Work 2 rows even in established rib patt (knit the knits and purl the purls as they appear), ending with a WS row—rib measures about ¾" (2 cm) from CO. Change to St st. Dec 1 st at each end of needle on next RS row, then work 3 rows even. Rep the last 4 rows 2 more times—61 (71, 81) sts rem. Work even for 4 rows—piece measures about 4" (10 cm) from CO. Inc 1 st at each end of needle on next RS row, then work 7 rows even. Rep the last 8 rows 2 more times—67 (77, 87) sts. Cont even until piece measures 10 (10½, 11)" (25.5 [26.5, 28] cm) from CO, ending with a WS row.

shape armholes

BO 5 (6, 7) sts at beg of next 2 rows—57 (65, 73) sts rem. DEC ROW: (RS) K2, k2tog, knit to last 4 sts ssk, k2—2 sts dec'd. Work 1 WS row even. Rep the shaping of the last 2 rows 1 (1, 2) more time(s)—53 (61, 67) sts rem. Rep the dec row, then work 3 rows even. Rep the last 4 rows 0 (1, 1) more time—51 (57, 63) sts rem. Work even until armholes measure 7 (7½, 8½)" (18 [19, 21.5] cm), ending with a WS row.

shape shoulders

BO 3 sts at beg next 6 rows, then BO 2 (3, 4) sts at beg of next 4 rows—25 (27, 29) sts rem. BO all sts.

RIGHT FRONT

CO 35 (40, 45) sts. NEXT ROW: (WS) *K2, p3; rep from * to end. Work 1 RS row in established rib. Work 1 WS row in rib, dec 1 st near center of row—34 (39, 44) sts rem; rib measures about ¾" (2 cm) from CO. Change to St st. Dec 1 st at end of needle (side edge) on next RS row, then work 3 rows even. Rep the last 4 rows 2 more times—31 (36, 41) sts rem. Work even for 4 rows—piece measures about 4" (10 cm) from CO. Inc 1 st at end of needle (side edge) on next RS row, then work 7 rows even. Rep the last 2 rows 2 more times—34 (39, 44) sts. Cont even until piece measures 10 (10½, 11)" (25.5 [26.5, 28] cm) from CO, ending with a RS row.

shape armhole

BO 5 (6, 7) sts at beg of next WS row—29 (33, 37) sts rem. DEC ROW: (RS) Knit to last 4 sts ssk, k2—1 st dec'd. Work 1 WS row even. Rep the shaping of the last 2 rows 1 (1, 2) more time(s)—27 (31, 34) sts rem. Rep the dec row, then work 3 rows even. Rep the last 4 rows 0 (1, 1) more time—26 (29, 32) sts rem. Work even until armhole measures 3½ (4, 4½)" (9 [10, 11.5] cm), ending with a WS row.

shape neck

NOTE: Work neck decs in the instructions below as foll: On RS rows, k2, k2tog, knit to end; on WS rows, purl to last 4 sts, p2tog, p2. Beg on the next RS row, dec 1 st at neck edge every row 4 (6, 8) times, then every other row 7 (6, 5) times, then every 4 rows 2 times—13 (15, 17) sts rem. Work even until armhole measures 9 (9½, 10)" (23 [24, 25.5] cm), ending with a WS row. BO all sts.

LEFT FRONT

CO 35 (40, 45) sts. NEXT ROW: (WS) *P3, k2; rep from * to end. Work 1 RS row in established rib. Work 1 WS row in rib, dec 1 st near center of row—34 (39, 44) sts rem; rib measures about ¾" (2 cm) from CO. Change to St st. Dec 1 st at beg of needle (side edge) on next RS row, then work 3 rows even. Rep the last 4 rows 2 more times—31 (36, 41) sts rem. Work even for 4 rows—piece measures about 4" (10 cm) from CO. Inc 1 st at beg of needle (side edge) on next RS row, then work 7 rows even. Rep the last 8 rows 2 more times—34 (39, 44) sts. Cont even until piece measures 10 (10½, 11)" (25.5 [26.5, 28] cm) from CO, ending with a WS row.

shape armhole

BO 5 (6, 7) sts at beg of next RS row—29 (33, 37) sts rem. DEC ROW: (RS) K2, k2tog, knit to end—1 st dec'd. Work 1 WS row even. Rep the shaping of the last 2 rows 1 (1, 2) more time(s)—27 (31, 34) sts rem. Rep the dec row, then work 3 rows even. Rep the last 4 rows 0 (1, 1) more time—26 (29, 32) sts rem. Work even until armhole measures 3½ (4, 4½)" (9 [10, 11.5] cm), ending with a WS row.

shape neck

NOTE: Work neck decs in the instructions below as foll: On RS rows, knit to last 4 sts, ssk, k2; on WS rows, p2, ssp (see Glossary), purl to end. Beg on the next RS row, dec 1 st

at neck edge every row 4 (6, 8) times, then every other row 7 (6, 5) times, then every 4 rows 2 times—13 (15, 17) sts rem. Work even until armhole measures 9 (9½, 10)" (23 [24, 25.5] cm), ending with a WS row. BO all sts.

SLEEVES (MAKE 2)

NOTE: Sleeve cuff is worked from side to side in cable patt, then sts are picked up along one selvedge of cuff and remainder of sleeve is worked in St st. CO 55 sts. NEXT ROW: (WS) K3 (rev St st edge sts), place marker (pm), work marked 26-st patt rep of Cable chart set-up row 2 times over next 52 sts. Keeping 3 edge sts in rev St st (purl on RS; knit on WS), rep Rows 1–24 of chart 2 times, then work Rows 1–6 once more—55 chart rows total including set-up row; piece measures about 11" (28 cm) from CO. BO all sts in patt on

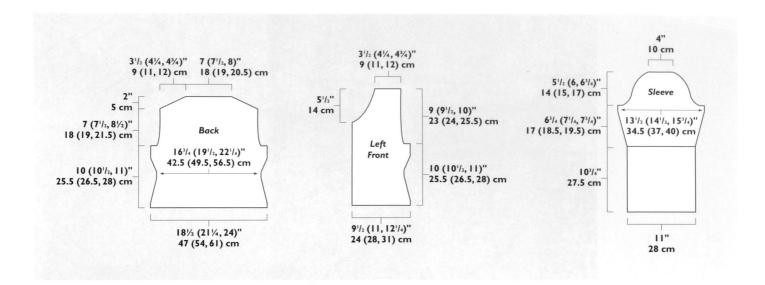

next RS row, dropping the sts that would ordinarily have been dropped in Row 10 and replacing them with yos as you BO—1 st rem on needle after last BO; do not cut yarn. With RS still facing, turn cuff so rev St st edge is across the top, then pick up and knit 42 sts evenly spaced along rev St st selvedge—43 sts total. Purl 1 WS row. Cont in St st, beg on the next RS row inc 1 st at each end of needle every 8 (6, 4) rows 3 (5, 7) times—49 (53, 57) sts. Cont even until piece measures 6¾ (7¼, 7¾)" (17 [18.5, 19.5] cm) from pick-up row and about 17½ (18, 18½)" (44.5 [45.5, 47] cm) from lower edge of sleeve for all sizes, ending with a WS row.

shape cap

BO 5 (6, 7) sts beg of next 2 rows—39 (41, 43) sts rem. DEC ROW: K2, k2tog, knit to last 4 sts, ssk, k2—2 sts dec'd. Purl 1 WS row. Rep the shaping of the last 0 (2, 2) rows 0 (1, 1) more time—37 (37, 39) sts rem. Rep dec row, then work 3 rows even. Rep the last 4 rows 4 (4, 5) more times—27 sts rem for all sizes. BO 3 sts at beg of next 4 rows—15 sts rem. BO all sts.

COLLAR

CO 119 sts. NEXT ROW: (WS) Work 15-st marked section of Cable chart set-up row once, then work marked 26-st patt rep a total of 4 times. Cont in patt, rep Rows 1–24 of chart 2 times, then work Rows 1 and 2 once more—51 chart rows total including set-up row; piece measures about 10¼" (26 cm) from pick-up row. BO all sts in patt on next RS row, dropping the sts that would ordinarily have been dropped in Row 10 and replacing them with yos as you BO.

FINISHING

Weave in loose ends. Block back, fronts, and sleeves to measurements.

With yarn threaded on a tapestry needle, use invisible horizontal seam (see Glossary) to sew straight shoulder edges of fronts to shaped shoulder edges of back. Sew sleeve caps into armholes, aligning center of each cap with top of armhole and not the shoulder seam (see Notes). Sew sleeve and side seams.

Pin collar in place so RS of collar corresponds to WS of garment in order for RS of collar to show on outside when collar is folded back, matching selvedges of collar to front edges and center of collar to center back neck. With yarn threaded on tapestry needle, sew collar to neck opening, easing collar to fit.

Using sewing needle and thread, sew zipper to front opening (see Glossary).

Lightly steam-block seams and collar, being careful not to flatten stitches.

Cable

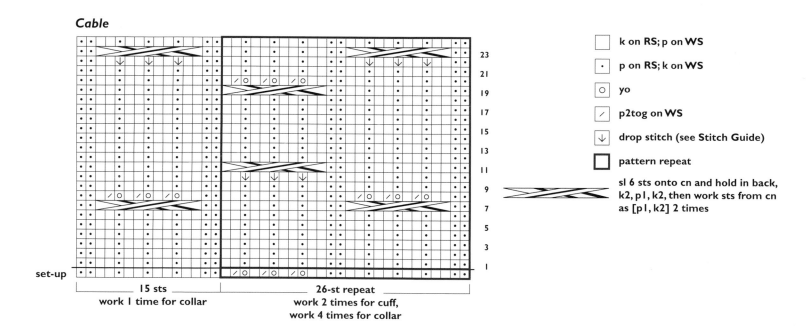

k on **RS**; p on **WS**

· p on **RS**; k on **WS**

○ yo

╱ p2tog on **WS**

↓ drop stitch (see **Stitch Guide**)

☐ pattern repeat

sl 6 sts onto cn and hold in back, k2, p1, k2, then work sts from cn as [p1, k2] 2 times

set-up

|__ 15 sts __|
work 1 time for collar

|____ 26-st repeat ____|
work 2 times for cuff,
work 4 times for collar

FINISHED SIZE

36½ (40, 44, 48)" (92.5 [101.5, 112, 122] cm) bust circumference, buttoned, with 1" (2.5 cm) front bands overlapped. Coat shown measures 36½" (92.5 cm).

YARN

Worsted weight (#4 Medium).

SHOWN HERE: Blue Sky Alpacas Worsted Hand Dyes (50% alpaca, 50% merino; 100 yd [91 m]/100 g): #2009 tan, 18 (20, 22, 24) skeins.

NEEDLES

Size 7 (4.5 mm). Adjust needle size if necessary to obtain the correct gauge.

NOTIONS

Markers (m); cable needle (cn); removable markers or waste yarn; tapestry needle; four ⅞" (2.2 cm) buttons; woven seam tape, sharp-point sewing needle and matching thread for attaching seam tape.

GAUGE

16½ stitches and 24 rows = 4" (10 cm) in stockinette stitch; 29-stitch pattern repeat from Rows 1–36 of both Lower Skirt and Sleeve charts measures 6½" (16.5 cm) wide; 26 stitches from Rows 1–40 of Side Gusset chart measure 6" (15 cm) wide; 53 stitches of Sleeve chart measure about 11¾" (30 cm) wide.

{ designer notes }

To add swing to the skirt, I added a side gore that tapered from the hem to the waist at each side. Doing so added at least 12 inches (30.5 centimeters) to the bottom circumference of the skirt, allowed the edges to meet gracefully at the center front, and added centered cable motifs along each side of the coat.

winter wonderland
COAT

I'm forever intrigued by the way bare tree branches against winter skies look like complex cable patterns. For this design, I wanted to create a sense of the trees' spare beauty in a long coat. The cable pattern is reminiscent of deciduous hardwoods with intertwining branches, and the intervening pointelle patterns suggest the orderly shapes of coniferous evergreens.

{ make it your own }

When things don't turn out as you plan, don't despair. Usually, you can find a creative solution. If a garment is too wide, add a belt or tie to gather in the excess fabric; if a garment is too narrow, add gores at the seams. There's a lot you can do to correct things without having to start over.

stitch guide

BOBBLE

Knit into the front, back, front of next st—3 sts made from 1. Turn, p3, turn, k3, turn, p3, turn sl 1 knitwise with yarn in back, k2tog, pass slipped st over—3 sts dec'd back to 1 st.

NOTE

¤ Because it contains so much yarn, this coat is heavy. Inevitably, it will grow as you wear it. To help prevent too much stretch at the shoulders, sew a strip of woven seam tape along the shoulder seams and across the back neck. Store the coat folded and flat on a shelf rather than hanging.

BACK

skirt

CO 111 (119, 140, 148) sts. Beg and ending with a WS row, knit 3 rows. Work 6 rows even in St st (knit RS rows; purl WS rows), ending with a WS row. Establish patt from Row 1 of Lower Skirt chart (page 62) on next row as foll: (RS) Beg and end as indicated for your size, work 12 (16, 12, 16) sts before patt rep box once, work 29-st patt rep 3 (3, 4, 4) times, work 12 (16, 12, 16) sts after patt rep box once. Cont in patt until Row 66 of chart has been completed, then work Rows 67–126 of Upper Skirt chart, working decs as shown—65 (73, 81, 89) sts rem; piece measures about 22" (56 cm) from CO.

bodice

Change to St st and work 2 rows even, ending with a WS row. NEXT ROW: (RS) K21 (23, 26, 28), place marker (pm), M1 (see Glossary), k23 (27, 29, 33), M1, pm, k21 (23, 26, 28)—67 (75, 83, 91) sts. Work 7 rows even in St st. INC ROW: (RS) Knit to first marker, slip marker (sl m), M1, knit to next marker, M1, sl m, knit to end—2 sts inc'd. Cont in St st, rep the shaping of the last 8 rows 2 more times—73 (81, 89, 97) sts. Work even until piece measures 6½ (6½, 7, 7½)" (16.5 [16.5, 18, 19] cm) from beg of St st bodice section, ending with a WS row.

shape armholes

BO 3 (3, 4, 5) sts at beg of next 2 rows, then BO 2 (3, 3, 4) sts at beg of foll 2 rows, then BO 1 st at beg of next 2 (2, 4,

4) rows—61 (67, 71, 75) sts rem. Work even until armholes measure 8 (8½, 9, 9½)" (20.5 [21.5, 23, 24] cm) and piece measures about 14½ (15, 16, 17)" (37 [38, 40.5, 43] cm) from beg of St st bodice section, ending with a WS row.

shape shoulders

Mark center 17 (19, 19, 21) sts with removable markers or waste yarn. NEXT ROW: (RS) BO 6 (6, 7, 7) sts, knit to marked center sts, join new yarn and BO center 17 (19, 19, 21) sts, knit to end. NEXT ROW: (WS) Working each side separately, BO 6 (6, 7, 7) sts at beg of first group of sts, purl to end of second group of sts—16 (18, 19, 20) sts rem at each side. Cont to work each side separately in St st, at each neck edge, BO 4 sts once, then BO 2 sts once, and *at the same time*, at each armhole edge, BO 5 (6, 7, 7) sts once, then BO 5 (6, 6, 7) sts once—no sts rem.

LEFT FRONT

skirt

CO 58 (62, 87, 91) sts. Beg and ending with a WS row, knit 3 rows. NEXT ROW: (RS) Knit to last 5 sts, pm, [k1, p1] 2 times, k1. NEXT ROW: (WS) [P1, k1] 2 times, p1, sl m, purl to end. Working 5 rib sts at front edge in established rib patt (knit the knits and purl the purls), work 4 rows even, ending with a WS row. Establish patt from Row 1 of Lower Skirt chart on next row as foll: (RS) Work 12 (16, 12, 16) sts before patt rep box once, work 29-st patt rep 1 (1, 2, 2) time(s), work 12 sts after patt rep box once for all sizes, sl m, work 5 front edge sts in established rib. Cont in patt until Row 66 of chart has been completed, then work Rows 67–126 of Upper Skirt chart, working decs as shown—38 (42, 54, 58) sts rem; piece measures about 22" (56 cm) from CO.

bodice

Maintaining 5 front edge sts rib patt, work rem sts in St st for 2 rows, dec 0 (0, 8, 8) sts evenly in St st section in first row—38 (42, 46, 50) sts rem. NEXT ROW: (RS) K21 (23, 26, 28), pm, M1, k12 (14, 15, 17), sl m, work 5 edge sts in rib—39 (43, 47, 51) sts. Work 7 rows even in St st. INC ROW: (RS) Knit to marker, sl m, M1, knit to last 5 sts, sl m, work 5 edge sts in rib—1 inc'd. Cont in patt, rep the shaping of the last 8 rows 2 more times—42 (46, 50, 54) sts. Work even until piece measures 5 (5, 5½, 6)" (12.5 [12.5, 14, 15] cm) from beg of St st bodice section, ending with a RS row.

shape neck and armhole

NOTE: Armhole shaping starts while neck shaping is in progress; read the next sections all the way through before proceeding. NEXT ROW: (WS) BO 5 front edge sts, purl to end—37 (41, 45, 49) sts rem. NEXT ROW: (RS) Knit to last 4 sts, ssk, k2—1 st dec'd at neck edge. Cont in St st, dec 1 st at neck edge in this manner every RS row 6 (7, 7, 7) more times, then every 4th row 6 (6, 6, 7) times, then every 6th row 2 times—20 (21, 21, 22) sts total removed at neck edge, including BO edge sts. *At the same time,* when St st section of bodice measures 6½ (6½, 7, 7½)" (16.5 [16.5, 18, 19] cm), shape armhole by BO at beg of RS rows 3 (3, 4, 5) sts once, then BO 2 (3, 3, 4) sts once, then BO 1 st 1 (1, 2, 2) time(s)—16 (18, 20, 21) sts rem when all neck and armhole

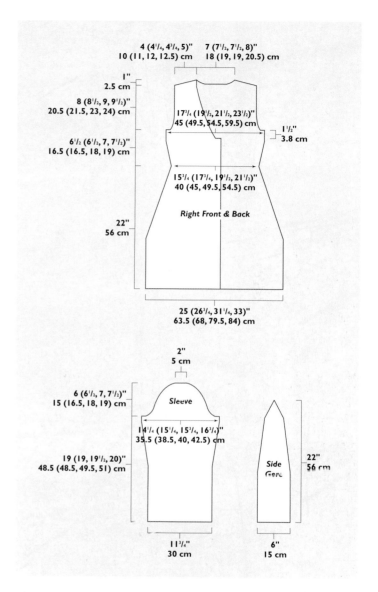

shaping has been completed. Work even until armhole measures 8 (8½, 9, 9½)" (20.5 [21.5, 23, 24] cm) and piece measures about 14½ (15, 16, 17)" (37 [38, 40.5, 43] cm) from beg of St st bodice section, ending with a WS row.

shape shoulder

BO 6 (6, 7, 7) sts at beg of next RS row, then BO 5 (6, 7, 7) sts at beg of foll RS row, then BO 5 (6, 6, 7) sts at beg of foll RS row—no sts rem.

Lower Skirt

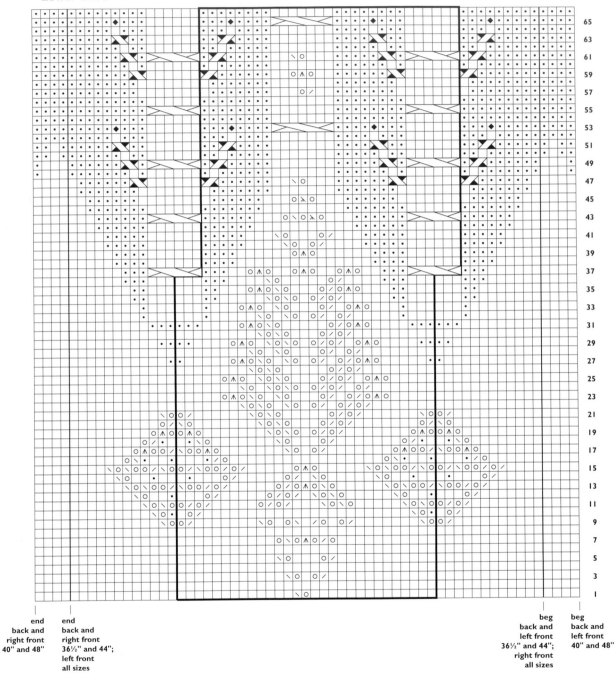

Upper Skirt

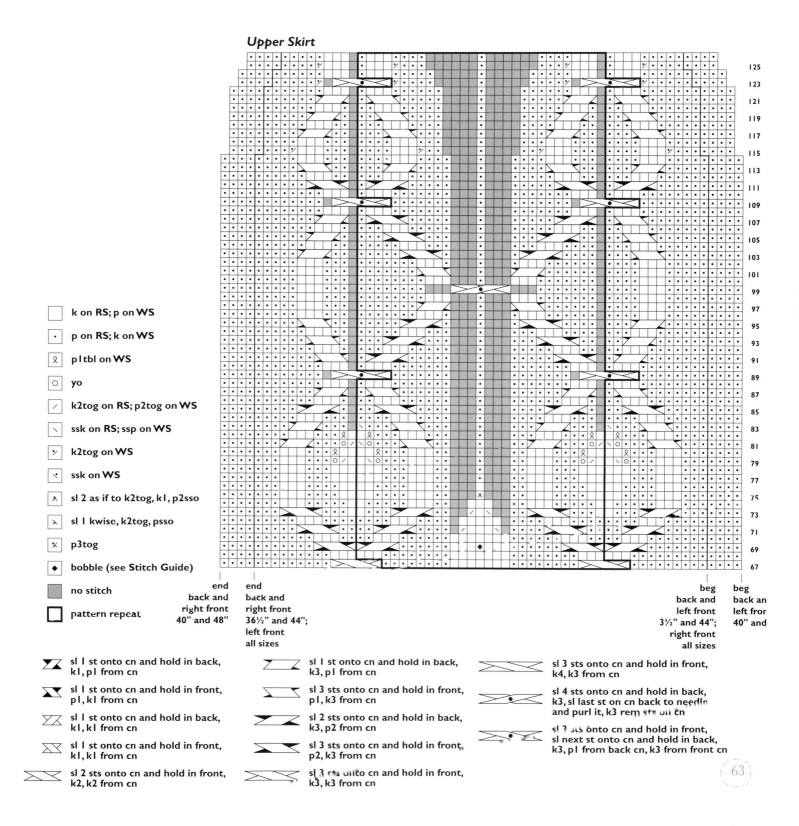

k on RS; p on WS

• p on RS; k on WS

℘ p1tbl on WS

○ yo

╱ k2tog on RS; p2tog on WS

╲ ssk on RS; ssp on WS

⟍ k2tog on WS

⟋ ssk on WS

⋀ sl 2 as if to k2tog, k1, p2sso

⋏ sl 1 kwise, k2tog, psso

⋉ p3tog

◆ bobble (see Stitch Guide)

▨ no stitch

▢ pattern repeat

end back and right front 40" and 48"

end back and right front 36½" and 44"; left front all sizes

beg back and left front 3½" and 44"; right front all sizes

beg back and left front 40" and

125
123
121
119
117
115
113
111
109
107
105
103
101
99
97
95
93
91
89
87
85
83
81
79
77
75
73
71
69
67

sl 1 st onto cn and hold in back, k1, p1 from cn

sl 1 st onto cn and hold in front, p1, k1 from cn

sl 1 st onto cn and hold in back, k1, k1 from cn

sl 1 st onto cn and hold in front, k1, k1 from cn

sl 2 sts onto cn and hold in front, k2, k2 from cn

sl 1 st onto cn and hold in back, k3, p1 from cn

sl 3 sts onto cn and hold in front, p1, k3 from cn

sl 2 sts onto cn and hold in back, k3, p2 from cn

sl 3 sts onto cn and hold in front, p2, k3 from cn

sl 3 sts onto cn and hold in front, k3, k3 from cn

sl 3 sts onto cn and hold in front, k4, k3 from cn

sl 4 sts onto cn and hold in back, k3, sl last st on cn back to needle and purl it, k3 rem sts on cn

sl 3 sts onto cn and hold in front, sl next st onto cn and hold in back, k3, p1 from back cn, k3 from front cn

Lower Gore

Upper Gore

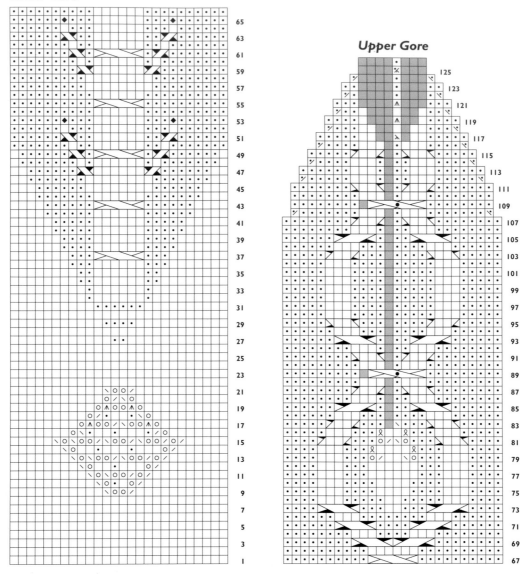

Sleeve

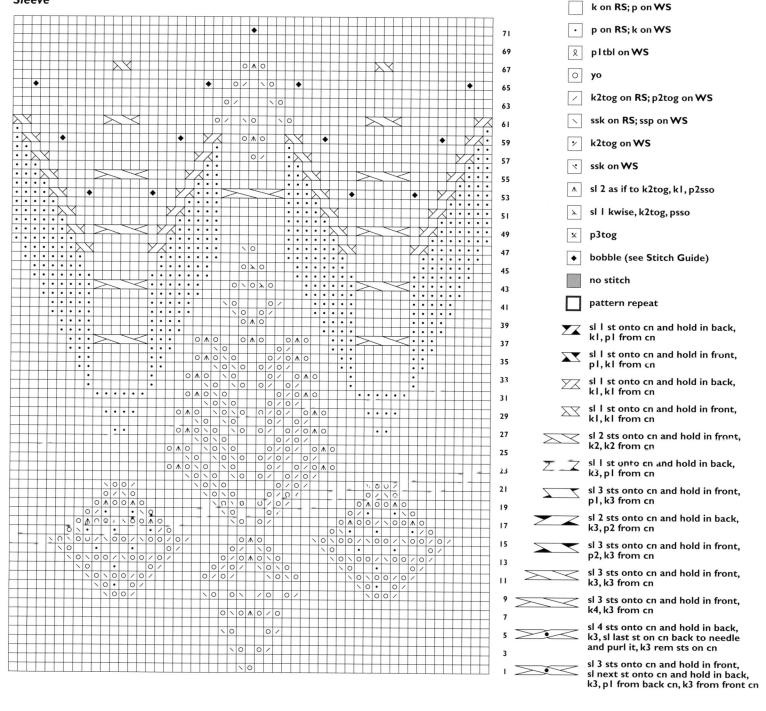

Legend:

☐ k on RS; p on WS

• p on RS; k on WS

℞ p1 tbl on WS

○ yo

╱ k2tog on RS; p2tog on WS

╲ ssk on RS; ssp on WS

⟍ k2tog on WS

⟋ ssk on WS

Λ sl 2 as if to k2tog, k1, p2sso

⅄ sl 1 kwise, k2tog, psso

⋉ p3tog

◆ bobble (see Stitch Guide)

▨ no stitch

☐ pattern repeat

⟍⟋ sl 1 st onto cn and hold in back, k1, p1 from cn

⟍⟋ sl 1 st onto cn and hold in front, p1, k1 from cn

⟍⟋ sl 1 st onto cn and hold in back, k1, k1 from cn

⟍⟋ sl 1 st onto cn and hold in front, k1, k1 from cn

⟍⟋ sl 2 sts onto cn and hold in front, k2, k2 from cn

⟍⟋ sl 1 st onto cn and hold in back, k3, p1 from cn

⟍⟋ sl 3 sts onto cn and hold in front, p1, k3 from cn

⟍⟋ sl 2 sts onto cn and hold in back, k3, p2 from cn

⟍⟋ sl 3 sts onto cn and hold in front, p2, k3 from cn

⟍⟋ sl 3 sts onto cn and hold in front, k3, k3 from cn

⟍⟋ sl 3 sts onto cn and hold in front, k4, k3 from cn

⟍⟋ sl 4 sts onto cn and hold in back, k3, sl last st on cn back to needle and purl it, k3 rem sts on cn

⟍⟋ sl 3 sts onto cn and hold in front, sl next st onto cn and hold in back, k3, p1 from back cn, k3 from front cn

RIGHT FRONT

skirt

CO 58 (62, 87, 91) sts. Beg and ending with a WS row, knit 3 rows. NEXT ROW: (RS) [K1, p1] 2 times, k1, pm, knit to end. NEXT ROW: (WS) Purl to last 5 sts, sl m, [p1, k1] 2 times, p1. Working 5 rib sts at front edge in established rib patt, work 4 rows even, ending with a WS row. Establish patt from Row 1 of Lower Skirt chart on next row as foll: (RS) Work 5 edge sts in established rib, sl m, work 12 sts before patt rep box once for all sizes, work 29-st patt rep 1 (1, 2, 2) time(s), work 12 (16, 12, 16) sts after patt rep box once. Cont in patt until Row 66 of chart has been completed, then work Rows 67–126 of Upper Skirt chart, working decs as shown—38 (42, 54, 58) sts rem; piece measures about 22" (56 cm) from CO.

bodice

With removable markers or waste yarn, mark positions of 4 buttons on left front edging, the lowest about ½" (1.3 cm) above end of upper skirt chart, the highest ½" (1.3 cm) below beg of neck shaping, and the rem 2 evenly spaced in between. Compare right and left fronts frequently as you work and make a 2-st one-row buttonhole (see Glossary) 2 sts in from the right front edge whenever the right front reaches the same length as a marked button position on the left front. Maintaining 5 front edge sts rib patt, work rem sts in St st for 2 rows, dec 0 (0, 8, 8) sts evenly in St st section in first row—38 (42, 46, 50) sts rem. NEXT ROW: (RS) Work 5 edge sts in rib, sl m, k12 (14, 15, 17), M1, pm, k21 (23, 26, 28)—39 (43, 47, 51) sts. Work 7 rows even in St st, including any required buttonholes. INC ROW: (RS) Work 5 edge sts in rib, sl m, knit to next marker, M1, sl m, knit to end—1 inc'd. Cont in patt and working buttonholes as required, rep the shaping of the last 8 rows 2 more times—42 (46, 50, 54) sts. Work even including any required buttonholes until piece measures 5 (5, 5½, 6)" (12.5 [12.5, 14, 15] cm) from beg of St st bodice section, ending with a WS row.

shape neck and armhole

NOTE: As for left front, armhole shaping starts while neck shaping is in progress; read the next sections all the way through before proceeding. NEXT ROW: (RS) BO 5 front edge sts, knit to end—37 (41, 45, 49) sts rem. Work 1 WS row even. NEXT ROW: (RS) K2, k2tog, knit to end—1 st dec'd at neck edge. Cont in St st, dec 1 st at neck edge in this manner every RS row 6 (7, 7, 7) more times, then every 4th row 6 (6, 6, 7) times, then every 6th row 2 times—20 (21, 21,

22) sts total removed at neck edge, including BO edge sts. *At the same time*, when St st section of bodice measures 6½ (6½, 7, 7½)" (16.5 [16.5, 18, 19] cm), shape armhole by BO at beg of WS rows 3 (3, 4, 5) sts once, then BO 2 (3, 3, 4) sts once, then BO 1 st 1 (1, 2, 2) time(s)—16 (18, 20, 21) sts rem when all neck and armhole shaping has been completed. Work even until armhole measures 8 (8½, 9, 9½)" (20.5 [21.5, 23, 24] cm) and piece measures about 14½ (15, 16, 17)" (37 [38, 40.5, 43] cm) from beg of St st bodice section, ending with a RS row.

shape shoulder

BO 6 (6, 7, 7) sts at beg of next WS row, then BO 5 (6, 7, 7) sts at beg of foll WS row, then BO 5 (6, 6, 7) sts at beg of foll WS row—no sts rem.

SIDE GORE (MAKE 2)

CO 26 sts. Beg and ending with a WS row, knit 3 rows. Work 6 rows even in St st, ending with a WS row. Work Rows 1–66 of Lower Gore chart, then work Rows 67–126 of Upper Gore chart, working decs as shown—1 st rem; piece measures about 22" (56 cm) from CO. BO rem st.

SLEEVES (MAKE 2)

CO 53 sts for all sizes. Beg with a WS row, knit 4 rows, then purl the foll WS row. Work Rows 1–62 of Sleeve chart—piece measures about 10" (25.5 cm) from CO. Cont to work center 53 sts in patt from chart, inc 1 st each end of needle on next RS row, then every foll 20 (10, 8, 6)th row 2 (4, 5, 7) more times, working new sts at each side in St st, then working all sts in St st after Row 72 of chart has been completed—59 (63, 65, 69) sts. Cont even in St st until piece measures 19 (19, 19½, 20)" (48.5 [48.5, 49.5, 51] cm) from CO, ending with a WS row.

shape cap

BO 3 (3, 4, 5) sts at beg of next 2 rows, then BO 2 (3, 3, 4) sts at beg of foll 2 rows—49 (51, 51, 51) sts rem. Dec 1 st each end of every RS row 14 (14, 11, 9) times, then dec 1 st each end of every other RS row 0 (1, 3, 5) time(s)—21 (21, 23, 23) sts rem. BO 2 (2, 3, 3) sts at beg of next 2 rows, then BO 4 sts at beg of foll 2 rows—9 sts rem. BO all sts.

COLLAR

CO 172 (182, 186, 194) sts.

ROWS 1 AND 3: (WS) P2, knit to last 2 sts, p2.

ROW 2: Knit.

ROW 4: (RS) K2, k2tog, k24 (26, 28, 30), *ssk, pm, k1, pm, k2tog,* k106 (112, 112, 116); rep from * to * once more, k24 (26, 28, 30), ssk, k2—166 (176, 180, 188) sts rem.

ROW 5: K3, purl to last 3 sts, k3.

ROW 6: K2, k2tog, *knit to 2 sts before m, ssk, sl m, k1, sl m, k2tog; rep from * once more; knit to last 4 sts, ssk, k2—6 sts dec'd.

ROWS 7–28: Rep Rows 5 and 6 eleven more times—94 (104, 108, 116) sts rem; piece measures about 4½" (11.5 cm) from CO measured straight up along a single column of sts; do not measure along diagonal dec lines. BO all sts.

FINISHING

Block pieces to measurements. Block collar flat with dec lines forming 45-degree angles; collar measures about 26 (27½, 27½, 28½)" (66 [70, 70, 72.5] cm) along CO edge between mitered corner sts, and 6¾ (7¼, 7¾, 8¼)" (17 [18.5, 19.5, 21] cm) along CO edge from each mitered corner st to selvedge. With yarn threaded on a tapestry needle, use the invisible horizontal seam (see Glossary) to join fronts to back at shoulders. Temporarily pin collar to neck opening with RS of collar corresponding to WS of garment so RS of collar will show on outside when collar is folded back, matching center of collar BO row to center back neck, and with selvedges of collar abutting where the 5-st front edgings were BO. Sew collar to body along neck opening and top of front edgings with RS facing so collar will conceal seam when folded to the outside.

Sew bodice side seams from base of armholes to top of charted skirt sections, leaving skirt free. Insert one side gore piece between the front and back skirts, aligning single st at top of side gore with bodice side seam. Sew gore to front and back. Sew second side gore in the same manner. Sew sleeve caps into armholes, easing to fit. Sew sleeve seams.

Sew buttons to marked positions on left front, opposite buttonholes. Weave in loose ends. Lightly steam-block seams and roll line of collar as needed, being careful not to flatten stitches.

design *workshop* #2

BUILDING A COLOR PALETTE

KNITWEAR DESIGNS INVOLVE COLOR, whether the particular colors are bold, saturated tones, quiet subtle neutrals, or something in between. Color is everywhere, but it takes a bit of effort to see the individual colors that make up a landscape, painting, or textile. If you enjoy working with color, you'll want to learn how to build a successful color palette. You don't need any special training—just look closely at the world around you and use the combinations that already exist in nature, art, and fashion. Notice the variety of vegetable-dyed colors in tapestries and carpets, the

vibrant hues of South American textiles, the earthy colors in Native American and primitive cave art, and the sun-drenched colors of a midday beach and you have some fine palettes to work with.

For example, if you imagine a palette inspired by a beach, you might think of beige sand, blue water, and gray rocks. This palette is workable but somewhat dull and lifeless. However, if you take a trip to the beach and look closely at actual colors, you'll find much more variety. If it's a sunny day, you'll find that the sand is speckled and heathered, and the water is grayish teal with shimmery gold dots where sunlight is reflected. The driftwood is a soft taupe, the sun-baked crab shells have a mellow peachy hue, the mussel shells are a chalky dark purple, and sea glass adds sparks of soft aqua and muted white. This "real" beach palette has a depth of color as well as some surprising accents that bring it to life. You can look closely at paintings, textiles, mosaics, or architecture in the same way for other inspired color combinations.

To create your own palette, you'll want lots and lots of small reelings or butterflies of yarn. This is where your yarn stash can come in handy—don't worry about fiber content or yarn weight,

just look for as many colors as you can find. You can augment your yarn stash with embroidery floss or needlepoint yarn, even paint chips from the hardware store (but be aware that you may not be able to find exactly the same colors in knitting yarn).

A workable color palette should have from six to sixteen colors. More than that will dilute the story. Besides, few of us want to manage more than sixteen colors. So, let's create a palette to go along with the mood board you created in Workshop #1 (page 22). Look at the colors in the pictures and objects on your mood board—is everything neutral creams, whites, and beiges? Are the colors mostly warm or cool? Pastel or saturated? Use your yarn reels, embroidery thread, and paint chips to make a palette (or two, or three) from the images on your board. Rearrange the colors to see which ones work well together and which ones don't. Notice how each color is affected by whatever colors are next to it. Try colors next to each other in different combinations to create completely different effects.

There are no "right" combinations, just combinations that look "right" to you.

FINISHED SIZE

43 (49, 55)" (109 [124.5, 139.5] cm) bust circumference. Sweater shown measures 49" (124.5 cm).

YARN

Chunky weight (#5 Bulky).

SHOWN HERE: Tahki Stacy Charles Baby (100% wool; 60 yd [55 m]/100 g): #18 camel, 12 (13, 15) balls.

NEEDLES

Body and sleeves—size 15 (10 mm): straight, 32" and 16" (60 and 40 cm) circular (cir), and set of 4 or 5 double-pointed (dpn). Collar—size 11 (8 mm): 16" (40 cm) cir. Adjust needle size if necessary to obtain the correct gauge.

NOTIONS

Markers (m); long stitch holder or spare 32" (60 cm) cir needle slightly smaller than larger needle to use as holder; tapestry needle.

GAUGE

8 stitches and 12 rounds = 4" (10 cm) in stockinette stitch, worked in rounds on larger needles.

{ designer notes }

I think of this kind of project as "comfort knitting." Much like "comfort food," it makes you feel warm, relaxed, and cozy. Except for a bit on the sleeves, there's no stitch pattern to track, and big needles make for quick progress. Even if you enjoy complicated patterns, it's nice to have a bit of "mindless" knitting: not much purling, no seaming, not much shaping, huge needles. Ahhh.

evergreen sleeve
TUNIC

This oversize tunic is all about fast and easy knitting and easy wearing. This warm sweater in the comforting color of a frothy cappuccino is just right to warm you up during the dead of winter. To avoid bulky seams, most of this sweater is knitted in the round.

{ make it your own }

Be sure to check your gauge as you knit this (or any) sweater. The bulky yarn used here knits up at just two stitches to the inch and a difference of even a quarter of a stitch per inch can add up to a lot of inches—and create a fabric that is either dreadfully loose and sloppy or horribly dense and stiff.

BODY
back

With larger straight needles, CO 42 (47, 52) sts. NEXT ROW: (WS) K2, *p3, k2; rep from * to end. Cont in established rib (knit the knits and purl the purls) until piece measures 6" (15 cm) from CO, ending with a RS row. NEXT ROW: (WS) Purl, inc 1 st at beg of row, 0 (0, 1) st in center, and 0 (1, 1) st at end of row—43 (49, 55) sts. Cut yarn and place sts on longer, larger cir needle.

front

CO and work as for back until rib measures 4" (10 cm) from CO, ending with a RS row. NEXT ROW: (WS) Purl, inc 1 st at beg of row, 0 (0, 1) st in center, and 0 (1, 1) st at end of row—43 (49, 55) sts. Do not cut yarn.

join front and back

With RS facing, sl 43 (49, 55) sts for front onto longer, larger cir needle without working them so first sts to be worked will be the front sts. JOINING RND: Knit across 43 (49, 55) front sts, place marker (pm) for side "seam," k43 (49, 55) back sts, pm for end of rnd—86 (98, 110) sts total. Knit 2 rnds. NEXT RND: *K3 (4, 4), [yo, ssk, k3] 8 (9, 10) times, k0 (0, 1), slip marker; rep from * once more. Cont in St st (knit all sts every rnd) until piece measures 16 (17, 18)" (40.5 [43, 45.5] cm) from front CO, or 18 (19, 20)" (45.5 [48.5, 51] cm) from back CO, ending last rnd 3 sts before end-of-rnd marker. NEXT RND: Removing markers as you come to them, BO last 3 sts of previous rnd, BO first 3 sts of this rnd, knit to 3 sts before side marker, BO 6 sts, knit to end—37 (43, 49) sts rem each for front and back. Place sts on long holder, waste yarn, or spare cir needle.

SLEEVES (MAKE 2)

With dpn, CO 27 (29, 31) sts. Pm and join for working in rnds, being careful not to twist sts. Knit 1 rnd, purl 1 rnd, knit 2 rnds. NEXT RND: K7 (8, 9), pm, work Rnd 1 of Sleeve chart over center 13 sts, pm, k7 (8, 9). Cont in patt from chart, working sts on each side of center panel in St st until piece measures 8" (20.5 cm) from CO. Cont chart patt as established, inc 1 st at each side of end of rnd marker on next rnd, work 10 rnds even, inc 1 st at each side of end of rnd marker on next rnd, changing to larger 16" (40 cm) cir needle if there are too many sts to fit around dpn—31 (33, 35) sts. Cont as established until Rnd 52 of chart has been completed, ending final rnd 3 sts before end of rnd marker—piece measures about 18¼" (46.5 cm) from CO for all sizes. NEXT RND: Removing end of rnd

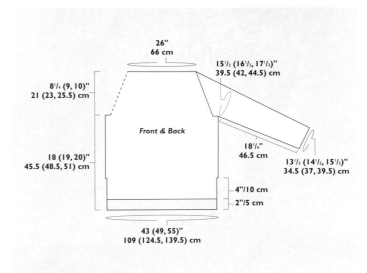

26"
66 cm

15½ (16½, 17½)"
39.5 (42, 44.5) cm

8¼ (9, 10)"
21 (23, 25.5) cm

Front & Back

18¼"
46.5 cm

13½ (14½, 15½)"
34.5 (37, 39.5) cm

18 (19, 20)"
45.5 (48.5, 51) cm

4"/10 cm

2"/5 cm

43 (49, 55)"
109 (124.5, 139.5) cm

marker as you come to it, BO last 3 sts of previous rnd, BO first 3 sts of this rnd, knit to end—25 (27, 29) sts rem.

YOKE

Join all sts onto longer, larger cir needle as foll: K25 (27, 29) left sleeve sts, pm, k37 (43, 49) front sts, pm, k25 (27, 29) right sleeve sts, pm, k37 (43, 49) back sts, pm to indicate end of rnd—124 (140, 156) sts total. DEC RND: *K1, k2tog, knit to 3 sts before marker, ssk, k1, slip m (sl m); rep from * 3 more times—8 sts dec'd. Knit 2 rnds even. Rep the shaping of the last 3 rnds 5 (2, 3) more times—76 (116, 124) sts; 25 (37, 41) sts each for front and back, 13 (21, 21) sts for each sleeve. Work dec rnd once more, then knit 1 rnd even—8 sts dec'd. Rep the shaping of the last 2 rnds 2 (7, 8) more times, changing to shorter larger cir needle when there are too few sts to fit around the longer cir needle. (NOTE: For the largest size there will only be 5 sleeve sts rem when you start the final dec rnd; for this size, work the sleeve sts in the last dec rnd as k1, sl 2 sts as if to k2tog, k1, pass 2 slipped sts over, k1.) When all yoke shaping has been completed—52 sts rem for all sizes; 19 (21, 23) sts each for front and back, 7 (5, 3) sts for

each sleeve. Knit 1 (2, 0) rnd(s)—yoke measures about 8¼ (9, 10)" (21 [23, 25.5] cm).

collar

Change to smaller cir needle and work k2, p2 ribbing until ribbing measures 3½" (9 cm). Knit 4 rnds even. Loosely BO all sts.

FINISHING

Weave in loose ends. With yarn threaded on a tapestry needle, sew BO sts tog at underarms. Lightly steam-block as needed.

Sleeve

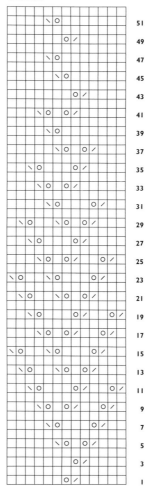

Symbol	Meaning
(blank)	knit
o	yo
/	k2tog
\	ssk

FINISHED SIZE

32½ (38½, 44, 49½)" (82.5 [98, 112, 125.5] cm) bust circumference, with 4½" (11.5 cm) wide front edgings overlapping about 2" (5 cm) at center front. Cardigan shown measures 38½" (98 cm). NOTE: Amount of overlap can be adjusted to accommodate larger, smaller, or in-between sizes.

YARN

Chunky weight (#5 Bulky) and DK weight (#3 Light).

SHOWN HERE: Reynolds Andean Alpaca Regal (90% alpaca, 10% wool; 110 yd (100 m)/100 g): #2 light gray (MC), 7 (8, 9, 10) balls.

Knit One Crochet Too Douceur et Soie (70% baby mohair, 30% silk; 225 yd [206 m]/ 25 g): #8918 fog (light gray, CC), 1 ball.

NEEDLES

Body and sleeves—size 10 (6 mm): 32" (80 cm) circular (cir). Edging—size 8 (5 mm): two 32" (80 cm) cir. Adjust needle size if necessary to obtain the correct gauge.

NOTIONS

Markers (m); cable needle (cn); stitch holders; tapestry needle.

GAUGE

14 stitches and 19 rows = 4" (10 cm) in stockinette stitch with MC on larger needle; 25 stitches of center sleeve chart measure 6¼" (16 cm) wide with MC on larger needle.

{ *designer notes* }

In this project, I mixed yarns of two different weights for the wispy mohair accent at the cuff. It's also okay to use a completely different needle size from the size suggested on the ball band— you might end up with surprisingly lovely results!

whisper cuff
CARDIGAN

This cardigan grew from my desire to use an unlikely yarn combination. I wanted to create a feminine garment with an elegant shape and delicate look, but I didn't want to have to knit a lot of lace on tiny needles. I decided to use common techniques in uncommon ways. It's anything but an ordinary knit!

{ *make it your own* }

Try experimenting with a finer mohair yarn or other fine yarns on larger needles in a variety of stitch patterns. Fine mohair gives a lovely, airy texture when knitted loosely—even in plain stockinette stitch.

NOTES

¤ The lower body is worked back and forth in rows in one piece to the armholes using a circular needle to accommodate the number of stitches, then divided and the fronts and back are worked separately to the shoulders.

¤ The ruffle that edges the neck, fronts, and hem is knitted in one piece around the entire body. Although it isn't all that big, it involves a lot of stitches. To make the knitting manageable, divide the stitches between two circular needles.

LOWER BODY

With larger needle and MC, CO 13 (15, 17, 19) sts for lower edge of center back. Work in St st beg with a WS purl row, and use the cable method (see Glossary) to CO 7 (8, 9, 10) sts at the end of the next 2 rows, then CO 6 (7, 8, 9) sts at the end of the foll 2 rows, then CO 5 (6, 7, 8) sts at the end of the foll 4 rows—59 (69, 79, 89) sts; piece measures about 1¾" (4.5 cm) from center back CO edge. NEXT ROW: (WS) P59 (69, 79, 89), place marker (pm) for right side "seam," CO 7 (9, 10, 12) sts for right front—66 (78, 89, 101) sts. NEXT ROW: (RS) K7 (9, 10, 12), slip m (sl m), k59 (69, 79, 89), pm for left side seam, CO 7 (9, 10, 12) sts for left front—73 (87, 99, 113) sts; 59 (69, 79, 89) back sts, 7 (9, 10, 12) sts each front. Slipping side m as you come to them, cont in St st and CO 3 (4, 6, 7) sts at the end of the next 2 rows, then CO 2 (3, 4, 5) sts at the end of the foll 2 rows, then CO 1 (2, 3, 4) st(s) at the end of the foll 2 rows—85 (105, 125, 145) sts; 59 (69, 79, 89) back sts; 13 (18, 23, 28) sts each front. Purl 1 WS row—piece measures about 3½" (9 cm) from center back CO edge.

shape waist and front edges

ROW 1: (RS) K1f&b (see Glossary), k5 (7, 10, 12), ssk, pm for right front dart, k5 (8, 10, 13), sl right side seam m, k15 (18, 21, 24), pm for right back dart, k2tog, k25 (29, 33, 37), ssk, pm for left back dart, k15 (18, 21, 24), sl left side seam m, k5 (8, 10, 13), pm for left front dart, k2tog, k5 (7, 10, 12), k1f&b—83 (103, 123, 143) sts rem; 57 (67, 77, 87) back sts, 13 (18, 23, 28) sts each front.

ROWS 2–4: Work even in St st.

ROW 5: (front inc row) K1f&b, knit to last st, k1f&b—1 st inc'd at each front edge.

ROWS 6 AND 8: Purl.

ROW 7: (waist dec row) Knit to 2 sts before right front dart

m, ssk, sl m, knit to right side seam m, sl m, knit to right back dart m, sl m, k2tog, knit to 2 sts before left back dart m, ssk, sl m, knit to left side seam m, sl m, knit to left front dart m, sl m, k2tog, knit to end—2 sts dec'd from back, 1 st dec'd from each front.

ROW 9: (front inc row) Rep Row 5—1 st inc'd at each front edge.

ROWS 10–12: Work even in St st.

ROW 13: (front inc and waist dec row) K1f&b, knit to 2 sts before right front dart m, ssk, sl m, knit to right side seam m, sl m, knit to right back dart m, sl m, k2tog, knit to 2 sts

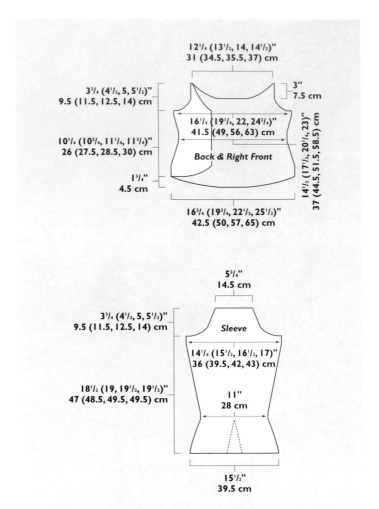

12¼ (13½, 14, 14½)"
31 (34.5, 35.5, 37) cm

3"
7.5 cm

3¾ (4½, 5, 5½)"
9.5 (11.5, 12.5, 14) cm

16¼ (19¼, 22, 24¾)"
41.5 (49, 56, 63) cm

10¼ (10¾, 11¼, 11¾)"
26 (27.5, 28.5, 30) cm

Back & Right Front

14½ (17½, 20¼, 23)"
37 (44.5, 51.5, 58.5) cm

1¾"
4.5 cm

16¾ (19¾, 22½, 25½)"
42.5 (50, 57, 65) cm

5¾"
14.5 cm

3¾ (4½, 5, 5½)"
9.5 (11.5, 12.5, 14) cm

Sleeve

14¼ (15½, 16½, 17)"
36 (39.5, 42, 43) cm

18½ (19, 19½, 19½)"
47 (48.5, 49.5, 49.5) cm

11"
28 cm

15½"
39.5 cm

Cuff

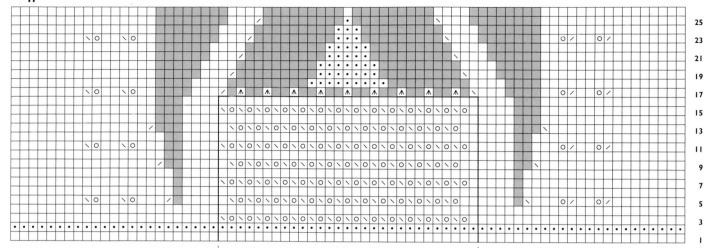

25
23
21
19
17
15
13
11
9
7
5
3
1

29 sts
work Rows 1–16 using CC

Edging

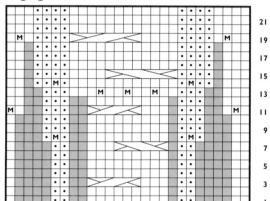

21
19
17
15
13
11
9
7
5
3
1

Center Sleeve

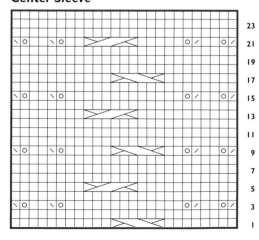

23
21
19
17
15
13
11
9
7
5
3
1

☐	k on RS; p on WS
•	p on RS; k on WS
O	yo
╱	k2tog
╲	ssk
⋀	sl 2 as if to k2tog, k1, p2sso
M	M1 (see Glossary)
▓	no stitch
☐	pattern repeat

sl 3 sts onto cn and hold in back, k3, k3 from cn

sl 3 sts onto cn and hold in front, k3, k3 from cn

sl 4 sts onto cn and hold in back, k4, k4 from cn

sl 4 sts onto cn and hold in front, k4, k4 from cn

before left back dart m, ssk, sl m, knit to left side seam m, sl m, knit to left front dart m, sl m, k2tog, knit to last st, k1f&b—1 st inc'd at each front edge, 2 sts dec'd from back, 1 st dec'd at each front dart.

ROWS 14–18: Work even in St st.

ROW 19: (waist dec row) Rep Row 7—77 (97, 117, 137) sts; 51 (61, 71, 81) back sts, 13 (18, 23, 28) sts each front.

ROWS 20–22: Work even in St st—piece measures about 8" (20.5 cm) from center back CO edge.

ROW 23: (RS, waist inc row) Knit to right front dart m, M1 (see Glossary), sl m, knit to right side m, sl m, knit to right back dart m, sl m, M1, knit to left back dart m, M1, sl m, knit to left side m, sl m, knit to left front dart m, sl m, M1, knit to end—2 sts inc'd for back, 1 st inc'd for each front.

ROWS 24–28: Work even in St st.

ROWS 29–34: Rep Rows 23–28 once more—2 sts inc'd for back, 1 st inc'd for each front.

ROW 35: (waist inc row) Rep Row 23—89 (109, 129, 149) sts; 57 (67, 77, 87) back sts, 16 (21, 26, 31) sts each front; piece measures about 10¾" (27.5 cm) from center back CO edge.

Work even in St st until piece measures 12 (12½, 13, 13½)" (30.5 [31.5, 33, 34.5] cm) from center back CO edge, ending with a WS row. **NEXT ROW:** (RS) K16 (21, 26, 31) for right front, place next 57 (67, 77, 87) sts on holder for back, then place rem 16 (21, 26, 31) sts on separate holder for left front.

RIGHT FRONT

NOTE: Armhole and neck shaping are worked at the same time; read all the way through the next section before proceeding. Working 16 (21, 26, 31) right front sts only, at armhole edge (beg of WS rows), BO 3 (4, 6, 7) sts once, then BO 2 (3, 4, 6) sts once, then BO 1 (2, 3, 4) st(s) once, then BO 1 st once—7 (10, 14, 18) sts total removed from armhole edge. *At the same time,* at neck edge (beg of RS rows), dec 1 st every RS row 9 (11, 12, 13) times—no sts rem when all armhole and neck shaping have been completed; armhole measures about 3¾ (4½, 5, 5½)" (9.5 [11.5, 12.5, 14] cm).

LEFT FRONT

Return 16 (21, 26, 31) held left front sts to larger needle and rejoin yarn with RS facing. **NOTE:** As for right front, armhole and neck shaping are worked at the same time; read all the

way through the next section before proceeding. Beg on the next RS row, at armhole edge (beg of RS rows), BO 3 (4, 6, 7) sts once, then BO 2 (3, 4, 6) sts once, then BO 1 (2, 3, 4) st(s) once, then BO 1 st once—7 (10, 14, 18) sts total removed from armhole edge. *At the same time,* at neck edge (end of RS rows), dec 1 st every RS row 9 (11, 12, 13) times—no sts rem when all armhole and neck shaping have been completed; armhole measures about 3¾ (4½, 5, 5½)" (9.5 [11.5, 12.5, 14] cm).

BACK

Return 57 (67, 77, 87) held back sts to larger needle and rejoin yarn with RS facing. **NOTE:** Armhole and neck shaping are worked at the same time; read all the way through the next section before proceeding. For armholes, BO 3 (4, 6, 7) sts at beg of next 2 rows, then BO 2 (3, 4, 6) sts at beg of foll 2 rows, then BO 1 (2, 3, 4) st(s) at beg of foll 2 rows, then BO 1 st at beg of foll 2 rows—14 (20, 28, 36) sts total removed by armhole shaping. *At the same time,* when armholes measure ¾ (1½, 2, 2½)" (2 [3.8, 5, 6.5] cm), place center 15 sts on holder, join new yarn, and working each side separately at each neck edge BO 5 (6, 7, 7) sts once, then BO 3 (4, 4, 5) sts once, then BO 2 sts 2 times, then BO 1 st 2 times—no sts rem after all armhole and neck shaping has been completed; armholes measure about 3¾ (4½, 5, 5½)" (9.5 [11.5, 12.5, 14] cm).

SLEEVES (MAKE 2)

NOTE: The lace insert in the center of the sleeve cuff is worked with CC using the intarsia method. Use a separate ball of MC at each side of the insert and twist the yarns at each color change to avoid leaving a hole. With larger needle, CO 23 sts with MC, then CO 29 sts with CC, then CO 23 sts with a separate ball of MC—75 sts total. Working each section with yarn indicated, work Rows 1–16 of Cuff chart. On Row 17, work across all sts in patt using a single ball of MC—49 sts rem. Work Rows 18–26 of chart—41 sts rem; piece measures about 5½" (14 cm) from CO in MC section. Establish patt from Row 1 of Center Sleeve chart on next row as foll: (RS) Work 8 sts in St st, pm, work 25 center sts in patt from chart, pm, work 8 sts in St st. Working sts at each side in St st, work Rows 2–24 of chart once, then rep Rows 1–24 to end of sleeve *and at the same time,* beg on the first Row 5 of center sleeve patt, inc 1 st each end of needle every 0 (6, 4, 4) rows 0 (5, 2, 5) times, then every 8 (8, 6, 6) rows 6 (3, 8, 6) times, working new sts in St st—53 (57, 61, 63) sts. Cont even until piece measures 18½ (19, 19½,

19½)" (47 [48.5, 49.5, 49.5] cm) from CO, ending with a WS row.

shape cap

BO 5 (5, 6, 6) sts at beg of next 2 rows, then BO 4 sts at beg of foll 2 rows, then BO 2 sts at beg of foll 2 rows—31 (35, 37, 39) sts rem. Dec 1 st at each end of needle on the next 4 (6, 7, 8) RS rows as foll: K1, k2tog, work in patt to last 3 sts, ssk, k1—23 sts rem for all sizes. Work 5 rows even in St st, ending with a WS row—cap measures about 3¾ (4½, 5, 5½)" (9.5 [11.5, 12.5, 14] cm) high. Place sts on holder.

FINISHING

Place held back neck and sleeve cap sts on waste yarn if necessary for blocking. Block pieces to measurements with a 7" (18 cm) gap between straight edges of fronts at center. NOTE: Edging is not shown on schematic and will add about 4½" (11.5 cm) to body length after finishing. With MC threaded on a tapestry needle, sew sleeves into armholes, leaving live sts at top of caps free.

cabled edging

With MC, smaller cir needle, RS facing, and beg at left back sleeve seam, k23 held left sleeve sts, pick up and knit 247 (259, 273, 303) sts evenly spaced around left front, back, and right front to right front sleeve seam, k23 held sts of right sleeve, pick up and knit 14 (16, 17, 18) sts along right back neck shaping, k15 held center back neck sts, and pick up and knit 14 (16, 17, 18) sts along left back neck shaping—336 (352, 368, 400) sts total. Pm for working in rnds, and divide sts on 2 smaller cir needles. Knit 2 rnds. Work Rnds 1–22 of Edging chart, inc 16-st patt rep to a 27-st rep as shown on chart—567 (594, 621, 675) sts after completing Rnd 22; edging measures about 4½" (11.5 cm) from pick-up rnd. BO all sts in patt.

Weave in loose ends. Lightly block seams as needed; avoid flattening the cabled edging.

FINISHED SIZE

36 (40½, 44, 48½)" (91.5 [103, 112, 123] cm) bust circumference. Sweater shown measures 40½" (103 cm).

YARN

Worsted weight (#4 Medium).

SHOWN HERE: Tahki Stacy Charles Torino (100% merino wool; 94 yd [86 m]/50 g): #107 chocolate brown (MC), 12 (13, 15, 16) balls; #112 denim blue (CC), 1 ball for all sizes.

NEEDLES

Size 7 (4.5 mm): straight and 16" and 32" (40 and 60 cm) circular (cir). Adjust needle size if necessary to obtain the correct gauge.

NOTIONS

Markers (m); stitch holders; cable needle (cn); tapestry needle; 10 grams of size 8 rocaille beads in clear pale blue; 5 grams each of size 8 rocaille beads in iridescent lavender and matte silver; small amounts of wool embroidery yarn or worsted-weight wool left-overs in an assortment of pale blues, lilacs, and creams; sharp-point sewing needle and thread to match MC for attaching beads.

GAUGE

18 stitches and 33 rows = 4" (10 cm) in seed stitch; 18 stitches and 24 rows = 4" (10 cm) in stockinette stitch; 6 stitch cable pattern measure about 1" (2.5 cm) wide.

{ designer notes }

When I add beads to my designs, I usually sew them on after the knitting is complete (rather than stringing them on the yarn and knitting them in place). That way, I have more freedom in where to put them.

frost flower cuff
PULLOVER

The embroidered flowers on the cuffs of this sweater remind me of frost patterns on windowpanes. Although flowers are typically not part of a winter landscape, you can find beautiful gardens in the miniscule world of crystalline ice that rival their showier summer counterparts.

{ make it your own }

This garment looks nice without embellishment—so don't feel obligated to add any. But if you do include the embroidery and beads, you'll need only small amounts of yarn. Check to see what you have in your stash before purchasing new balls.

stitch guide

SEED STITCH (ODD NUMBER OF STS)

ALL ROWS: *K1, p1; rep from * to last st, k1.

Repeat this row for pattern.

RIGHT CABLE (WORKED OVER 6 STS)

RNDS 1–3: P1, k4, p1.

RND 4: P1, sl 2 sts onto cn and hold in back of work, k2, k2 from cn, p1.

RNDS 5 AND 6: Rep Rnd 1.

Repeat Rnds 1–6 for pattern.

LEFT CABLE (WORKED OVER 6 STS)

RNDS 1–3: P1, k4, p1.

RND 4: P1, sl 2 sts onto cn and hold in front of work, k2, k2 from cn, p1.

RNDS 5 AND 6: Rep Rnd 1.

Repeat Rnds 1–6 for pattern.

BACK

With CC and straight needles, CO 77 (87, 95, 105) sts. Beg and ending with a WS row, work 3 rows in St st (knit RS rows; purl WS rows). Change to MC and knit 1 row. Beg on the next WS row, work even in seed st (see Stitch Guide) for 10 rows—piece measures about 1¾" (4.5 cm) from CO with lower edge unrolled. DEC ROW: (RS) Dec 1 st each end of needle—2 sts dec'd. Work 9 rows even in seed st, then rep dec row once more—73 (83, 91, 101) sts rem. Work even in seed st until piece measures 5" (12.5 cm) from CO with lower edge unrolled, ending with a WS row. INC ROW: (RS) Inc 1 st each end of needle—2 sts inc'd. Work 7 rows even in seed st, working new sts into seed st patt. Cont in patt, rep the shaping of the last 8 rows 2 more times, then work inc row once more—81 (91, 99, 109) sts. Work even until piece measures 9½ (10, 10¼, 10½)" (24 [25.5, 26, 26.5] cm) from CO, ending with a WS row.

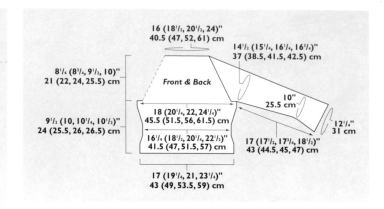

shape armholes

BO 4 (5, 5, 6) sts at beg of next 2 rows—73 (81, 89, 97) sts rem. Place sts on holder.

FRONT

CO and work as for back. Place sts on separate holder.

SLEEVES (MAKE 2)

With CC and straight needles, CO 55 sts for all sizes. Purl 1 WS row, then knit the next 4 rows, ending with a WS row. Change to MC and knit 1 RS row. Work 3 rows even in St st, ending with a WS row. DEC ROW: (RS) Ssk, knit to last 2 sts, k2tog—2 sts dec'd. Work 5 rows even in St st. Rep the shaping of the last 6 rows once more, then rep dec row—49 sts. Purl 1 WS row. Work Rows 1–24 of Sleeve chart, dec 1 st each end of needle on Rows 5 and 11 as shown on chart—45 sts rem. Working all sts in seed st, work even until piece measures 7½" (19 cm) from CO, ending with a WS row. INC ROW: (RS) Inc 1 st each end of needle—2 sts inc'd. Work 5 rows even in seed st, working new sts into seed st patt. Cont in patt, rep the shaping of the last 6 rows 8 (10, 12, 13) more times, then work inc row once more—65 (69, 73, 75) sts. Work even until piece measures 17 (17½, 17¾, 18½)" (43 [44.5, 45, 47] cm) from CO, ending with a WS row.

shape cap

BO 4 (5, 5, 6) sts at beg of next 2 rows—57 (59, 63, 63) sts rem. Place sts on holder.

YOKE

With RS facing, transfer sts to longer cir needle in the foll order: 57 (59, 63, 63) left sleeve sts, pm, 73 (81, 89, 97) front sts, pm, 57 (59, 63, 63) right sleeve sts, pm, 73 (81, 89, 97) back sts, pm to indicate end of rnd—260 (280, 304, 320) sts. Join for working in the rnd and rejoin MC so beg of rnd is at beg of left sleeve sts. Establish cable patts on next rnd as foll: *Work right cable (see Stitch Guide) over 6 sts, work in established seed st to 6 sts before marker (m), work left cable over 6 sts; rep from * 3 more times. Working 6 sts at each end of every marked section in cable patts and working sts in between in seed st, work 2 (2, 2, 8) rnds even. DEC RND: *Work 6 sts in cable patt, work either ssk or ssp (see Glossary) as needed to match seed st patt, work in seed st to 8 sts before m, k2tog or p2tog as needed to match seed st patt, work 6 sts in cable patt; rep from * 3 more times—8 sts dec'd. Work 2 rnds even in patt. Rep the shaping of the last 3 rnds 20 (21, 23, 23) more times, then work dec rnd once more, changing to shorter cir needle when necessary—84 (96, 104, 120) sts rem; 29 (35, 39, 47) sts each for front and back, 13 sts for each sleeve—yoke measures about 8¼ (8¾, 9½, 10)" (21 [22, 25, 25.5] cm) from joining rnd.

collar

Cont in established patts for 12 more rnds. Change to CC and knit 1 rnd, purl 1 rnd, knit 3 rnds—collar measures about 2½" (6.5 cm) high. With CC, BO all knitwise.

FINISHING

Weave in loose ends. With yarn threaded on a tapestry needle, sew sleeve and side seams. Sew BO sts tog at underarms. With WS facing, lightly steam-block seams as needed, being careful not to flatten sts.

embroidery

Using wool embroidery yarn or other leftover yarn, embroider daisy stitches (see Glossary) on St st section of lower sleeves as shown below. With sharp-point sewing needle and thread, sew a cluster of either 4 iridescent lavender or 4 matte silver beads in the center of each flower. Sew clear pale blue beads to St st section randomly scattered around flowers as shown below.

Lower sleeve embroidery and bead placement.

Sleeve

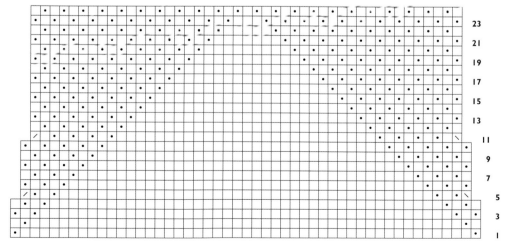

23
21
19
17
15
13
11
9
7
5
3
1

☐ k on RS; p on WS

· p on RS; k on WS

⁄ k2tog

⧵ ssk

spring

Spring's freshness and its lengthening days inspire knitting that's light, both in color and texture. Crisp greens, whites, ivories, and shades of pink erupt all around. The dainty first flowers of spring, wet with drops of rain, shift my design sense to all things light, wispy, and feminine. I turn to open, airy stitches in fresh pastel colors as buds bloom and delicate ferns unfurl their new leaves. Spring is definitely the time for knitting lace.

After I've been cooped up inside for many months, *March* brings on the urge to do spring cleaning, inside and out. In the garden, the remnants of last year's blossoms and leaves are dried and faded. Their skeletal shapes are beautiful, resembling bits of Victorian lace (both knitted and crocheted) that I treasure. Handed down by my grandmother and unknown ancestors from both sides of my family, the lace inspires all sorts of design ideas.

In *April,* the light begins to change, and quite suddenly, the days are long again. Bright light streams in through the windows. It filters through my grandmother's lace curtains, which now hang in my windows and create beautiful patterns on the floor. I always marvel at the thought that someone made them by hand using such fine crochet cotton. Can I use the same fine cotton in a knitted design to capture a similar look?

In *May,* spring truly arrives at my home in Maine. Flowers burst forth, birds build nests and lay beautifully colored eggs, grass turns green, forsythia bushes become fountains of yellow blossoms, and the branches of cherry and crabapple trees are thick with fragrant blooms. The days are warmer but evenings can remain quite chilly. Little cardigans, shrugs, stoles, and lightweight wraps are perfect to wear. Again, I look to the flowers for inspiration. I like to add embroidery in bits of light-colored yarns to suggest the look of cherry blossoms or flowering vines—no heavy intarsia here.

Look closely at the shapes and colors of spring flowers, birds, and insects to get ideas for embroidery and lace accents to add to your own knitting projects.

FINISHED SIZE

36 (40, 44½, 49)" (91.5 [101.5, 113, 124.5] cm) bust circumference, with about a 1" to 2" (2.5 to 5 cm) gap between neck edgings at center front. Shrug shown measures 40" (101.5 cm). **NOTE:** Amount of gap at center front can be adjusted to accommodate larger, smaller, or in-between sizes.

YARN

Worsted weight (#4 Medium).

SHOWN HERE: Manos del Uruguay Wool (100% wool; 135 yd [123 m]/100 g): #33 butane (MC, seafoam), 5 (5, 6, 7) skeins.

Knit One Crochet Too Ambrosia (70% alpaca, 20% silk, 10% cashmere; 137 yd (125 m)/50 g): #841 fawn (beige), 1 (1, 2, 2) balls

NEEDLES

Body and sleeves—size 8 (5 mm). Edging—size 4 (3.5 mm): straight and two 32" (80 cm) circular (cir). Adjust needle size if necessary to obtain the correct gauge.

NOTIONS

Markers (m); tapestry needle.

GAUGE

15 stitches and 22 rows = 4" (10 cm) in stockinette stitch with MC and larger needles; 38 stitches of Lily of the Valley pattern from chart measure 9½" (24 cm) wide with MC and larger needles.

{ designer notes }

This stitch pattern creates uneven edges that would be awkward in a sweater knitted from the bottom up. But when turned 45 degrees, the uneven edges create built-in shaping.

lily of the valley
SHRUG

The idea for this sweater came from a swatch I knitted of a stitch pattern that created alternating "swooshes" and "swoops" punctuated by little pointelle holes. What came to mind were tiny flowers hanging from curved stems surrounded by smooth-edged veined leaves—quite a bit like the lilies of the valley in my garden. The perfect pattern for a spring sweater!

{ make it your own }

I used a much finer yarn and a contrasting color to add a feminine ruffle around the edges of this shrug. But if you prefer something less frilly or don't want to introduce a second yarn, work a round of single crochet with the main color followed by a round of reverse single crochet.

stitch guide

CENTERED DOUBLE DECREASE (CDD)

Sl 2 sts as if to k2tog, k1, pass 2 slipped sts over—3 sts dec'd to 1 st.

NECK EDGING (MULTIPLE OF 6 STS, INC'D TO MULTIPLE OF 14 STS)

RND 1: Purl.

RND 2: *K1, yo, k5, yo; rep from * to end—patt rep inc'd to multiple of 8 sts.

RNDS 3, 5, 7, AND 9: Knit.

RND 4: *K2, yo, k1, CDD (see above), k1, yo, k1; rep from * to end.

RND 6: *K1, p1, k1, yo, CDD, yo, k1, p1; rep from * to end.

RND 8: *K1, p2, k1, yo, k1, yo, k1, p2; rep from * to end—patt rep inc'd to multiple of 10 sts.

RND 10: *[K2, yo] 2 times, k3, yo, k2, yo, k1; rep from * to end—patt rep inc'd to multiple of 14 sts.

RND 11: Knit.

SLEEVE EDGING (MULTIPLE OF 6 STS + 1, INC'D TO MULTIPLE OF 14 STS + 1)

SET-UP ROW: (WS) Knit.

ROW 1: (RS) *K1, yo, k5, yo; rep from * to last st, k1—patt rep inc'd to multiple of 8 sts plus 1.

ROWS 2, 4, 6, AND 8: Purl.

ROW 3: *K2, yo, k1, CDD, k1, yo, k1; rep from * last st, k1.

ROW 5: *K1, p1, k1, yo, CDD, yo, k1, p1; rep from * to last st, k1.

ROW 7: *K1, p2, k1, yo, k1, yo, k1, p2; rep from * last st, k1—patt rep inc'd to multiple of 10 sts plus 1.

ROW 9: *[K2, yo] 2 times, k3, yo, k2, yo, k1; rep from * to last st, k1—patt rep inc'd to multiple of 14 sts plus 1.

ROW 10: Purl.

NOTES

¤ The cast-on and neck edges of the back are worked straight across while on the needles, but the lily-of-the-valley pattern will naturally curve the fabric to create the effect of a shaped lower edge and back neck.

¤ Each front is worked from side to side with the cast-on along the front edge and the bind-off at the side seam and armhole edge. As for the back, these edges are worked straight across while on the needles, but the lily-of-the-valley pattern will naturally curve the fabric to create the effect of rounded front edges and a suggestion of armhole shaping. The schematic shows the right front oriented as it will appear when worn, with an arrow indicating the direction of the knitting.

¤ The sleeves are worked from the top of the sleeve cap down to the cuff. Like the back and fronts, the top and bottom edges are worked straight across while on the needles, but will curve naturally into the shapes shown after binding off. The schematic shows the sleeve oriented in the direction of the knitting, with the cast-on sleeve cap edge at the bottom; it does not include the sleeve edging.

¤ If during shaping there are not enough stitches to work a decrease with its companion yarnover from the Lily-of-the-Valley chart, work the stitches in stockinette instead to avoid throwing off the stitch count. There are 10 stitches between each decrease/yarnover pair, so you will need to check on each side of the 10 separating stitches to see if you need to omit a decrease or yarnover because there are not enough stitches to work its companion.

BACK

With MC and larger needles, CO 70 (78, 86, 94) sts. SET-UP ROW: (RS) K16 (20, 24, 28), place marker (pm), work Row 1 of Lily-of-the-Valley chart over center 38 sts, pm, k16 (20, 24, 28). Working sts at each side in St st (knit RS rows; purl WS rows), cont in patt as established until piece measures 3 (3½, 3¾, 4)" (7.5 [9, 9.5, 10] cm) from CO, ending with a WS row.

shape armholes

Cont in patt, BO 2 (3, 4, 5) sts at beg of next 2 rows (see Notes)—66 (72, 78, 84) sts rem. DEC ROW: (RS) K2, k2tog, work in patt to last 4 sts, ssk, k2—2 sts dec'd. Dec 1 st each end of needle in this manner every RS row 3 (4, 6, 7) more times—58 (62, 64, 68) sts rem. Cont even until armholes measure 7 (7, 7½, 8)" (18 [18, 19, 20.5] cm), ending with a WS row.

shape shoulders

BO 3 (3, 3, 4) sts at beg of next 4 rows, then BO 3 (3, 4, 4) sts at beg of next 2 rows—40 (44, 44, 44) sts rem. BO rem sts.

FRONT (MAKE 2)

With MC and larger needles, CO 42 (44, 46, 50) sts. SET-UP ROW: (RS) K2 (3, 4, 6), pm, work Row 1 of Lily-of-the-Valley chart over center 38 sts, pm, k2 (3, 4, 6). Working sts at each side in St st, cont in patt as established until piece measures 7 (8, 9¼, 10¼)" (18 [20.5, 23.5, 26] cm) from CO, ending with a WS row and measuring straight up from deepest point of curve in center of CO edge. BO all sts.

SLEEVES (MAKE 2)

With MC and larger needles, CO 62 (62, 66, 70) sts. SET-UP ROW: (RS) K12 (12, 14, 16), pm, work Row 1 of Lily-of-the-Valley chart over center 38 sts, pm, k12 (12, 14, 16). Working sts at each side in St st, cont in patt as established until piece measures 1½ (2, 3, 3½)" (3.8 [5, 7.5, 9] cm) from CO, ending with a WS row. Cont in patt, dec 1 st each end of needle, then work 9 (11, 9, 9) rows even—2 sts dec'd. Cont in patt, rep the shaping of the last 10 (12, 10, 10) rows 9 (8, 9, 10) more times—42 (44, 46, 48) sts rem. Cont even until piece measures 22½ (23, 23½, 24½)" (57 [58.5, 59.5, 62] cm) from CO or 1¼" (3.2 cm) less than desired length to end of sleeve edging, measuring straight up from deepest point of curve in center of CO edge, ending with a WS row. BO all sts.

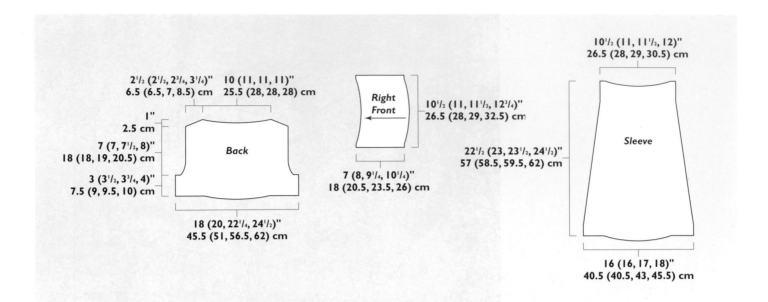

2¹⁄₂ (2¹⁄₂, 2³⁄₄, 3¹⁄₄)"
6.5 (6.5, 7, 8.5) cm

10 (11, 11, 11)"
25.5 (28, 28, 28) cm

1"
2.5 cm

7 (7, 7¹⁄₂, 8)"
18 (18, 19, 20.5) cm

3 (3¹⁄₂, 3³⁄₄, 4)"
7.5 (9, 9.5, 10) cm

Back

18 (20, 22¹⁄₄, 24¹⁄₂)"
45.5 (51, 56.5, 62) cm

Right Front

10¹⁄₂ (11, 11¹⁄₂, 12³⁄₄)"
26.5 (28, 29, 32.5) cm

7 (8, 9¹⁄₄, 10¹⁄₄)"
18 (20.5, 23.5, 26) cm

10¹⁄₂ (11, 11¹⁄₂, 12)"
26.5 (28, 29, 30.5) cm

Sleeve

22¹⁄₂ (23, 23¹⁄₂, 24¹⁄₂)"
57 (58.5, 59.5, 62) cm

16 (16, 17, 18)"
40.5 (40.5, 43, 45.5) cm

Lily of the Valley

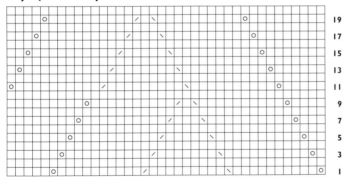

19
17
15
13
11
9
7
5
3
1

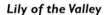

- ☐ k on RS; p on WS
- ⊙ yo
- ╱ k2tog
- ╲ ssk

FINISHING

Lightly steam-block pieces to measurements.

Place back on a flat surface with WS facing up. Lay the fronts RS up on top of back, aligning the front BO edges with the side edges of back and with curved CO edges of fronts at center. With MC threaded on a tapestry needle, sew BO edge of each front to straight side edge of back for 3 (3½, 3¾, 4)" (7.5 [9, 9.5, 10] cm) to beg of back armhole shaping, leaving rem BO edge of front free. Align upper selvedges of fronts with back shoulders. With MC threaded on a tapestry needle and working from the outer edges of each back shoulder in toward the center, sew fronts to back at shoulders for about 2½ (2½, 2¾, 3¼)" (6.5 [6.5, 7, 8.5] cm).

neck edging

With CC, smaller cir needle, RS facing, and beg at right shoulder seam, pick up and knit 50 (54, 54, 54) sts across back neck (about 5 sts for every 4 back neck sts), 60 (66, 72, 79) sts along curved CO edge of left front to beg of straight selvedge at lower left front, 21 (24, 28, 32) sts across left front selvedge to side seam, 70 (78, 88, 96) sts across back lower edge to side seam, 21 (24, 28, 32) sts across right lower selvedge to beg of curved CO edge, and 60 (66, 72, 79) sts along curved CO edge of right front to shoulder seam—282 (312, 342, 372) sts total. Pm and join for working in rnds. Work Rnds 1–11 of neck edging (see Stitch

Guide), dividing sts on 2 cir needles when there are too many sts to fit comfortably on one needle—658 (728, 798, 868) sts; neck edging measures about 1¼" (3.2 cm) from pick-up rnd at deepest point. BO all sts.

sleeve edging

With CC, smaller straight needles, and RS facing, pick up and knit 43 (49, 55, 61) sts across BO edge of sleeve. Working back and forth in rows, work the set-up row and Rows 1–10 of sleeve edging (see Stitch Guide)—99 (113, 127, 141) sts; sleeve edging measures about 1¼" (3.2 cm) from pick-up row at deepest point. BO all sts.

With yarn threaded on a tapestry needle, sew CO edge of sleeves into armhole openings, matching center of sleeve to shoulder seam and easing to fit. Sew sleeve seams. Weave in loose ends. Block lightly again if desired.

FINISHED SIZE

36 (40½, 44½, 48)" (91.5 [103, 113, 122] cm) bust circumference. Sweater shown measures 44½" (113 cm).

YARN

DK weight (#3 Light).

SHOWN HERE: Classic Elite Premiere (50% cotton, 50% Tencel; 108 yd [99 m]/ 50 g): #5226 tidal wave (aqua; MC), 8 (9, 11, 12) skeins.

DMC Baroque Crochet Cotton Size 10 (100% mercerized cotton; 400 yd [366 m]/about 1½ oz): ecru (CC), 1 (1, 1, 2) skeins.

NEEDLES

Body and sleeves—size 6 (4 mm). Scarf collar—size 5 (3.75 mm). Adjust needle size if necessary to obtain the correct gauge.

NOTIONS

Markers (m); stitch holders; tapestry needle; size D/3 (3.25 mm) crochet hook.

GAUGE

17½ stitches and 29 rows = 4" (10 cm) with MC in seed stitch on larger needles; 25 stitches and 32 rows = 4" (10 cm) with CC in collar pattern on smaller needles, after blocking.

{ designer notes }

This garment turned out to be looser than I expected, and the seed stitch made it a bit heavier than if it had been knitted in stockinette stitch. Although the fronts and back were shaped at the waist, the sweater tended to hang straight from the shoulders. To solve the problem, I added narrow ties at the back that, by happy coincidence, accentuated the curved back hemline with soft gathers.

seed-stitch
POET JACKET

From a woven jacket with an attached scarf in an upscale boutique, I got the idea of using a contrasting lace "scarf" as a collar on a romantic knitted cardigan. I envisioned a fitted silhouette in a soft drapey fabric. To give the sweater a bit of body, I worked it in seed stitch. I used crochet cotton yarn to give the attached scarf a Victorian feel.

{ make it your own }

The lace pattern I chose for the scarf is a simple one. But you could substitute any pattern that will repeat evenly into about the same number of stitches. Or, make a second piece of the same lace, attach a buckle to one end, and you've got a great vintage-style belt.

stitch guide

SELVEDGE STITCHES

Unless otherwise specified (as for front edges), on RS rows slip the first st pwise with yarn in back (wyb) and knit the last st; on all WS rows, slip the first st pwise with yarn in front (wyf) and purl the last st.

SEED STITCH (ODD NUMBER OF STS)

ALL ROWS: *P1, k1; rep from * to last st, p1.

Repeat this row for pattern.

SEED STITCH (EVEN NUMBER OF STS)

ROW 1: *P1, k1; rep from * to end.

ROW 2: *K1, p1; rep from * to end.

Repeat Rows 1 and 2 for pattern.

LACE PATTERN (MULTIPLE OF 10 STS + 1)

ROW 1: (RS) *P1, k2, yo, ssk, p1, k2tog, yo, k2; rep from * to last st, p1.

ROWS 2 AND 4: (WS) *K1, p4; rep from * to last st, k1.

ROW 3: *P1, k2tog, yo, k2, p1, k2, yo, ssk; rep from * to last st, p1.

Repeat Rows 1–4 for pattern.

NOTE

¤ This project is deliberately worked at a looser gauge than is typical for DK weight yarn in order to create a fabric with luxurious drape.

BACK

With MC, larger needles, and using the long-tail method (see Glossary), CO 27 (29, 33, 37) sts. Slipping the first st and working the last st for selvedge sts, work 1 WS row even in seed st (see Stitch Guide). Working new sts into seed st patt and maintaining selvedge sts as much as possible, use the backward-loop method (see Glossary) to CO 4 sts at end of next 10 (12, 16, 14) rows, then CO 3 sts at end of next 4 (4, 0, 4) rows—79 (89, 97, 105) sts. Work even in patt for 6 more rows, ending with a WS row—piece measures about 3 (3¼, 3¼, 3½)" (7.5 [8.5, 8.5, 9] cm) from CO at center. DEC ROW: (RS) Sl 1, ssk, work in patt to last 3 sts, k2tog, k1—2 sts dec'd. Work 7 rows even. Cont in patt, rep the shaping of the last 8 rows 4 more times—69 (79, 87, 95) sts rem. Work 2" (5 cm) even in patt—piece measures about 10½ (10¾, 10¾, 11)" (26.5 [27.5, 27.5, 28] cm) from CO at center, ending with a WS row. INC ROW: (RS) Sl 1, M1 (see Glossary) either kwise or pwise to maintain seed st patt, work in patt to last st, M1, k1—2 sts inc'd. Working new sts into patt, work 5 rows even. Cont in patt, rep the shaping of the last 6 rows 4 more times—79 (89, 97, 105) sts. Work even until piece measures 16 (16½, 17, 17½)" (40.5 [42, 43, 44.5] cm) from CO at center, ending with a WS row.

shape armholes

Dec 1 st each end of needle inside selvedge sts every row 6 (6, 8, 8) times—67 (77, 81, 89) sts. Dec 1 st each end of needle every 3 rows 3 (5, 5, 7) times—61 (67, 71, 75) sts rem. Cont even in patt until armholes measure 7½ (8, 8½, 9)" (19 [20.5, 21.5, 23] cm), ending with a WS row.

shape neck and shoulders

Keeping in patt, work 23 (25, 26, 27) sts, join new ball of yarn and BO center 15 (17, 19, 21) sts, work in patt to end—23 (25, 26, 27) sts rem each side. Working each side separately, dec 1 st at each neck edge every row 5 times and *at the same time*, at each armhole edge BO 4 (5, 5, 5) sts once, then BO 4 (5, 5, 6) sts 2 times, then BO 6 (5, 6, 5) sts once—no sts rem.

RIGHT FRONT

NOTE: Work 3 front edge sts in St st throughout (k3 at beg of RS rows; p3 at end of WS rows); do not slip any sts along front edge, but do maintain the selvedge st at side edge (end of RS rows; beg of WS rows). With MC, larger needles, and using the long-tail method, CO 5 (6, 8, 10) sts. NEXT ROW: (WS) Sl 1 (selvedge st), work in seed st to last 3 sts, place marker (pm), p3 (front edge sts). NOTE: Front and lower edge shaping are worked at the same time; read all the way through the next section before proceeding. Working new sts into seed st patt and maintaining selvedge st as much as possible, use the backward-loop method to CO 4 sts at end of next 5 (6, 8, 7) RS rows, then CO 3 sts at end of foll 2 (2, 0, 2) RS rows, then work 7 rows even, ending with a

WS row—26 (30, 32, 34) sts total added at lower edge; 21 (23, 23, 25) rows completed, including starting WS row. *At the same time*, beg on the next WS row, inc 1 st at front edge every other WS row inside edge sts 5 (5, 5, 6) times as foll: (WS) Work in patt to last 3 sts, M1 either kwise or pwise to maintain seed st patt, sl m, p3—5 (5, 5, 6) sts total added at front edge; 36 (41, 45, 50) sts when all side CO and front incs have been completed; piece measures about 3 (3¼, 3¼, 3½)" (7.5 [8.5, 8.5, 9] cm) from CO at center. NOTE: Waist decs are worked at the same time as front shaping cont; read all the way through the next section before proceeding. Beg on the next RS row, dec 1 st every 8 rows 5 times as foll: (RS) K3 (edge sts), work in patt to last 3 sts, k2tog, k1—5 sts total removed at side by waist shaping. *At the same time* cont to inc 1 st at front edge inside m every 4th row as established 3 (3, 3, 2) more times—3 (3, 3, 2) sts more added at front edge; 34 (39, 43, 47) sts when all waist decs and front shaping have been completed. Work even in patt until piece measures about 10½ (10¾, 10¾, 11)" (26.5 [27.5, 27.5, 28] cm) from CO, ending with a WS row. INC ROW: (RS) K3, sl m, work in patt to last st, M1, k1—1 st inc'd at side. Working new st into patt, work 5 rows even. Cont in patt, rep the shaping of the last 6 rows 4 more times—39 (44, 48, 52) sts. Work even until piece measures 16 (16½, 17, 17½)" (40.5 [42, 43, 44.5] cm) from CO, ending with a WS row.

shape armhole and neck

NOTE: Neck and armhole shaping are worked at the same time; read all the way through the next section before proceeding. Dec 1 st at neck edge inside edge sts every 4 rows 12 (13, 14, 15) times as foll: (RS) K3, sl m, ssk, work in patt to end including any required armhole shaping. *At the same time* dec 1 st at armhole edge (end of RS rows; beg of WS rows) every row 6 (6, 8, 8) times, then every 3 rows 3 (5, 5, 7) times—9 (11, 13, 15) sts total removed at armhole edge; 18 (20, 21, 22) sts rem when all neck and armhole shaping have been completed. Cont even in patt until armhole measures 7½ (8, 8½, 9)" (19 [20.5, 21.5, 23] cm), ending with a RS row.

shape shoulder

BO at 4 (5, 5, 5) sts at beg of next WS row, then BO 4 (5, 5, 6) sts at beg of foll 2 WS rows, then BO 6 (5, 6, 5) sts at beg of foll WS row—no sts rem.

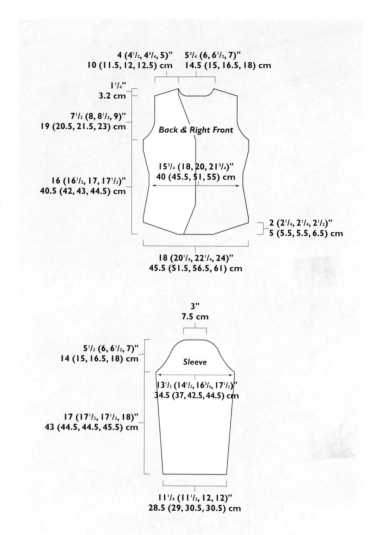

4 (4½, 4¾, 5)"   5¾ (6, 6½, 7)"
10 (11.5, 12, 12.5) cm   14.5 (15, 16.5, 18) cm

1¼"
3.2 cm

7½ (8, 8½, 9)"
19 (20.5, 21.5, 23) cm

Back & Right Front

15¾ (18, 20, 21¾)"
40 (45.5, 51, 55) cm

16 (16½, 17, 17½)"
40.5 (42, 43, 44.5) cm

2 (2¼, 2¼, 2½)"
5 (5.5, 5.5, 6.5) cm

18 (20¼, 22¼, 24)"
45.5 (51.5, 56.5, 61) cm

3"
7.5 cm

5½ (6, 6½, 7)"
14 (15, 16.5, 18) cm

Sleeve

13½ (14½, 16¾, 17½)"
34.5 (37, 42.5, 44.5) cm

17 (17½, 17½, 18)"
43 (44.5, 44.5, 45.5) cm

11¼ (11½, 12, 12)"
28.5 (29, 30.5, 30.5) cm

LEFT FRONT

NOTE: Work 3 front edge sts in St st throughout (k3 at end of RS rows; p3 at beg of WS rows); do not slip any sts along front edge, but do maintain the selvedge st at side edge (beg of RS rows; end of WS rows). With MC, larger needles, and using the long-tail method, CO 5 (6, 8, 10) sts. NEXT ROW: (WS) P3 (front edge sts), pm, work in seed st to last st, p1 (selvedge st). NOTE: Front and lower edge shaping are worked at the same time as for right front; read all the way through the next section before proceeding. Working new sts into seed st patt and maintaining selvedge st as much as possible, using the backward-loop method, CO 4 sts at beg of next 5 (6, 8, 7) RS rows, then CO 3 sts at beg of foll 2 (2, 0, 2) RS rows, then work 7 rows even, ending with a WS row—26 (30, 32, 34) sts total added at lower edge; 21 (23, 23, 25) rows completed, including starting WS row. *At the same time,* beg on the next WS row, inc 1 st at front edge every other WS row inside edge sts 5 (5, 5, 6) times as foll: (WS) P3, sl m, M1 either kwise or pwise to maintain seed st patt, work in patt to end—5 (5, 5, 6) sts total added at front edge; 36 (41, 45, 50) sts when all side CO and front incs have been completed; piece measures about 3 (3¼, 3¼, 3½)" (7.5 [8.5, 8.5, 9] cm) from CO at center. NOTE: Waist decs are worked at the same time as front shaping cont; read all the way through the next section before proceeding. Beg on the next RS row, dec 1 st every 8 rows 5 times as foll: (RS) Sl 1, ssk, work in patt to last 3 sts, k3—5 sts total removed at side by waist shaping. *At the same time* cont to inc 1 st at front edge inside m every 4th row as established 3 (3, 3, 2) more times—3 (3, 3, 2) sts more added at front edge; 34 (39, 43, 47) sts when all waist decs and front shaping have been completed. Work even in patt until piece measures about 10½ (10¾, 10¾, 11)" (26.5 [27.5, 27.5, 28] cm) from CO, ending with a WS row. INC ROW: (RS) Sl 1, M1 either kwise or pwise to maintain seed st patt, work in patt to last 3 sts, k3—1 st inc'd at side. Working new st into patt, work 5 rows even. Cont in patt, rep the shaping of the last 6 rows 4 more times—39 (44, 48, 52) sts. Work even until piece measures 16 (16½, 17, 17½)" (40.5 [42, 43, 44.5] cm) from CO, ending with a WS row.

shape armhole and neck

NOTE: Neck and armhole shaping are worked at the same time; read all the way through the next section before proceeding. Dec 1 st at neck edge inside edge sts every 4 rows 12 (13, 14, 15) times as foll: (RS) Work in patt to last 5 sts including any required armhole shaping, k2tog, sl m, k3. *At the same time* dec 1 st at armhole edge (beg of RS rows; end of WS rows) every row 6 (6, 8, 8) times, then every 3 rows 3 (5, 5, 7) times—9 (11, 13, 15) sts total removed at armhole edge; 18 (20, 21, 22) sts rem when all neck and armhole shaping have been completed. Cont even in patt until armhole measures 7½ (8, 8½, 9)" (19 [20.5, 21.5, 23] cm), ending with a WS row.

shape shoulder

BO 4 (5, 5, 5) sts at beg of next RS row, then BO 4 (5, 5, 6) sts at beg of foll 2 RS rows, then BO 6 (5, 6, 5) sts at beg of foll RS row—no sts rem.

SLEEVES (MAKE 2)

With MC, larger needles, and using the long-tail method, CO 49 (51, 53, 53) sts. Slipping the first st and working the last st for selvedge sts, work 6 rows even in seed st, ending with a WS row. INC ROW: (RS) Sl 1, M1 either kwise or pwise to maintain patt, work in patt to last st, M1, k1—2 sts inc'd. Working new sts into patt, work 19 (17, 11, 9) rows even. Cont in patt, rep the shaping of the last 20 (18, 12, 10) rows 4 (5, 9, 11) more times—59 (63, 73, 77) sts. Cont even in patt until piece measures 17 (17½, 17½, 18)" (43 [44.5, 44.5, 45.5] cm) from CO, ending with a WS row.

shape cap

Keeping in patt, dec 1 st each end of needle inside selvedge sts every row 6 (6, 8, 8) times, then every 3 rows 3 (5, 5, 7) times—41 (41, 47, 47) sts rem. Dec 1 st each end of needle every other row 11 (9, 7, 5) times, then every row 3 (5, 10, 12) times—13 sts rem for all sizes. BO all sts.

SCARF COLLAR

With CC, smaller needles, and using the long-tail method, CO 43 sts. Working 1 selvedge st at each end of row as for body, rep Rows 1–4 of lace patt (see Stitch Guide) over center 41 sts until piece measures 57 (58½, 60, 61½)" (145 [148.5, 152.5, 156] cm) from CO, ending with a WS row. BO all sts in patt.

FINISHING

Block pieces to measurements, blocking scarf collar to about 7" (18 cm) wide and 57 (58½, 60, 61½)" (145 [148.5, 152.5, 156] cm) long. With MC threaded on a tapestry needle, sew fronts to back at shoulders. Sew sleeve caps into armholes. Sew sleeve and side seams.

waist ties (make 2)

With MC and crochet hook, chain (ch) 134 (154, 170, 184) (see Glossary for crochet instructions). NEXT ROW: Work 1 single crochet (sc) in each ch. Fasten off, leaving a long tail for attaching tie. With tail threaded on a tapestry needle, sew one tie to each side seam, even with topmost waist dec row, at the start of the waist section worked even.

attach scarf collar

Mark center of collar and align with center back neck. With CC threaded on a tapestry needle, sew collar to neck opening, beg at center back and ending at start of neck shaping, allowing ends of scarf collar to hang loose as shown.

front ties (make 2)

With MC and crochet hook, make a chain about 11" (28 cm) long. Fasten off. Sew one tie to WS of each front selvedge just below start of neck shaping, underneath the scarf collar. Weave ties in and out of yarnover holes in scarf collar. To wear, tie at center front, gathering collar at base of neck V.

Weave in loose ends. Steam-block seams as needed. Tie waist ties loosely at center back.

Bear Claw

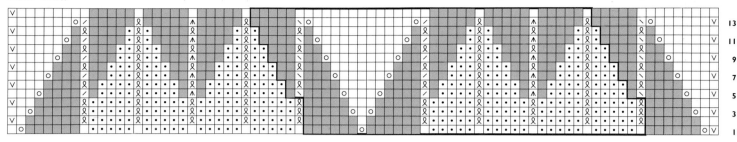

Lace Insert

Sleeve Diamond

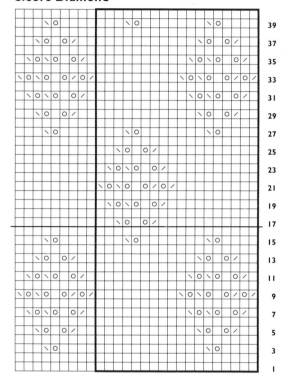

shape shoulders

Working each side separately in St st, at each armhole edge BO 6 (7, 8, 8) sts 2 times, then BO 6 (7, 7, 8) sts once, then BO rem 7 sts.

SLEEVES (MAKE 2)

CO 75 (75, 89, 89) sts. Knit 1 WS row. Establish patt from Row 1 of Cuff chart as foll: (RS) Work 9 sts before patt rep box once, work 14-st patt rep 4 (4, 5, 5) times, work 10 sts after patt rep box once. Work Rows 2–39 of chart, ending with a RS row. Purl 1 WS while row dec 0 (0, 3, 3) sts evenly spaced—75 (75, 86, 86) sts rem. Establish patt from Lace Insert chart as foll: (RS) Work selvedge st before patt rep box once, rep 11-st patt 6 (6, 7, 7) times, work 8 sts after patt rep box once. Rep Rows 1–4 of Lace Insert chart until piece measures about 6 (6½, 6½, 7)" (15 [16.5, 16.5, 18] cm) from CO, ending with Row 4 of chart. NEXT ROW: (RS) Sl 1, purl to last st, k1. NEXT ROW: (WS) Sl 1, purl to end. NEXT ROW: (RS) Sl 1, knit to end while inc 2 (2, 4, 4) sts evenly spaced—77 (77, 90, 90) sts. NEXT ROW: (WS) Sl 1, knit to last st, p1. Establish patt from Zigzag chart as foll: (RS) Sl 1 (selvedge st), work 2 sts in St st, rep 13-st patt 5 (5, 6, 6) times, work 6 sts after patt rep box once, work 2 sts in St st, k1 (selvedge st). Work Rows 2–38 of chart and *at the same time* inc 1 st at each side inside selvedge sts on Rows 5, 9, 13, 17, 21, 25, 29, 33, and 37, working new sts in St st—95 (95, 108, 108) sts. Work bobble band as foll:

ROWS 1 AND 5: (RS) Sl 1 (selvedge st), purl to last st, k1 (selvedge st).

ROWS 2 AND 4: Sl 1, purl to end.

⬜	k on RS; p on WS	
•	p on RS; k on WS	
ℛ	k1tbl on RS; p1tbl on WS	
○	yo	
╱	k2tog on RS; p2tog on WS	
╲	ssk on RS; ssp on WS	
⋏	sl 1 st kwise, k2tog, psso	

⋀	centered double dec
v	sl 1
⬛	bobble
▨	no stitch
⬜	pattern repeat
⧄	sl 2 sts onto cn and hold in back k2, k2 from cn
⧅	sl 2 sts onto cn and hold in front, k2, k2 from cn

103

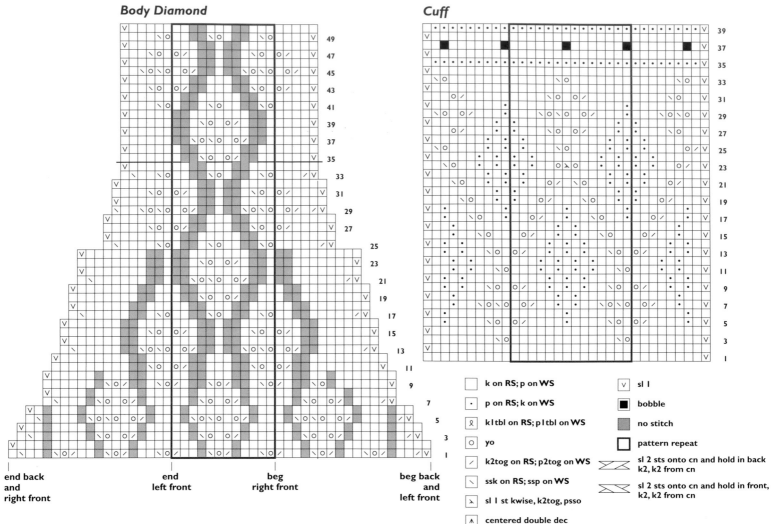

Body Diamond

Cuff

☐ k on RS; p on WS	V sl 1
· p on RS; k on WS	■ bobble
ℓ k1tbl on RS; p1tbl on WS	▨ no stitch
○ yo	☐ pattern repeat
⁄ k2tog on RS; p2tog on WS	⤬ sl 2 sts onto cn and hold in back k2, k2 from cn
＼ ssk on RS; ssp on WS	⤬ sl 2 sts onto cn and hold in front, k2, k2 from cn
⋏ sl 1 st kwise, k2tog, psso	
⋀ centered double dec	

end back and right front · end left front · beg right front · beg back and left front

ROW 3: Sl 1, M1, k7 (7, 6, 6), *work bobble in next st, k6; rep from * to last 3 sts, k2, M1, k1—97 (97, 110, 110) sts.

ROW 6: Sl 1, purl to end, inc 8 (8, 1, 1) st(s) evenly spaced—105 (105, 111, 111) sts; piece measures about 10¼ (10¾, 10¾, 11¼)" (26 [27.5, 27.5, 28.5] from CO.

Establish patt from Sleeve Diamond chart as foll: (RS) Sl 1 (selvedge st), work 11 (11, 14, 14) sts in St st, work 18-st patt rep 4 times, work 9 sts after patt rep box once, work 11 (11, 14, 14) sts in St st, k1 (selvedge st).

size 32" only

Work Rows 2–22 of chart, and beg on Row 3, inc 1 st at each

side inside selvedge sts every 4 rows 5 times, working new sts into sleeve diamonds patt—115 sts; piece measures about 12½" (31.5 cm) from CO. Skip to Shape Cap below.

size 36" only

Work Rows 2–24 of chart, and beg on Row 3 inc 1 st at each side inside selvedge every RS row 4 times, then every other RS row 3 times, working new sts into sleeve diamonds patt—119 sts; piece measures about 13" (33 cm) from CO. Skip to Shape Cap below.

Small Ruffle

(chart)

11
9
7
5
3
1

Large Ruffle

(chart)

15
13
11
9
7
5
3
1

Zigzag

(chart)

37
35
33
31
29
27
25
23
21
19
17
15
13
11
9
7
5
3
1

(selvedge st)—2 sts dec'd. Cont in patt, rep dec row on next 15 (16, 15, 16) RS rows—73 sts rem for all sizes. Maintaining selvedge sts, work even in patt until cap measures 6 (6½, 6¾, 7)" (15 [16.5, 17, 18] cm), ending with a WS row. Work decs to gather top of cap as foll:

ROW 1: (RS) Sl 1, k16, [CDD (see Stitch Guide), k4] 2 times, CDD, k5, CDD, [k4, CDD] 2 times, k17—61 sts rem.

ROWS 2 AND 4: Sl 1, purl to end.

ROW 3: Sl 1, k15, [CDD, k2] 2 times, CDD, k3, CDD, [k2, CDD] 2 times, k16—49 sts rem.

ROW 5: Sl 1, k14, [CDD] 3 times, k1, [CDD] 3 times, k15—37 sts rem.

ROW 6: Rep Row 2.

BO 6 sts at beg of next 4 rows—13 sts rem; cap measures about 7 (7½, 7¾, 8)" (18 [19, 19.5, 20.5] cm). BO all sts.

FINISHING

upper bodice ruffle

With RS of front facing and beg at left armhole edge, use cir needle to pick up all the single strands between the eyelet holes in the single diagonal eyelet line above the vertical patts of the front; these strands are just slipped onto the needle, not picked up and knitted. Make a note of the number of picked-up sts on needle. With dpn, CO 8 sts for ruffle. SET-UP ROW: (WS) K1, p6, purl the last ruffle st tog with first st on cir needle at left armhole edge—still 8 ruffle sts; 1 picked-up st joined. Work sts on dpn in patt from Small Ruffle chart, and working last st of every WS row as p2tog to join last ruffle st to next picked-up st on cir needle, rep Rows 1–12 of chart until all picked-up sts have been joined. NOTE: If the original number of picked-up sts on the cir needle was not a multiple of 6 sts + 1, you will need to "fudge" the join in order to have the ruffle end with Row 12. Determine how many more sts you would have needed to reach the next multiple of 6 sts + 1, and on that many evenly spaced WS ruffle rows omit the join and simply work the last ruffle st as p1. When all picked-up sts have been joined, BO ruffle sts.

lower bodice ruffles

left ruffle

With RS of front facing and beg at left armhole edge, use cir needle to pick up 1 strand from every row along the line of purl sts dividing beg of front chart from body diamond patt at left front (the purl sts between the front cable and the dia-

size 41" only

Work Rows 2–28 of chart, and beg on Row 3 inc 1 st at each side inside selvedge sts every other RS row 6 times, working new sts into sleeve diamonds patt—123 sts; piece measures about 13½" (34.5 cm) from CO. Skip to Shape Cap below.

size 46" only

Work Rows 2–28 of chart, inc 1 st at each side inside selvedge sts every RS row 9 times, working new sts into sleeve diamonds patt—129 sts; piece measures about 14" (35.5 cm) from CO.

shape cap

NOTE: After working to Row 40 of Sleeve Diamond chart once, for rem of sleeve cap rep only Rows 17–40 of chart; do not rep Rows 1–16. When sleeve cap measures 5½ (6, 6¼, 6½)" (14 [15, 16, 16.5] cm) high, finish any diamond motifs in progress, but do not start any new diamond motifs to prevent having partial motifs at top of cap; work sts in St st after completing final diamonds. BO 5 (6, 9, 11) sts at beg of next 2 rows—105 (107, 105, 107) sts. DEC ROW: (RS) Sl 1 (selvedge st), k2tog, work in patt to last 3 sts, ssk, k1

Front Rows 51–168

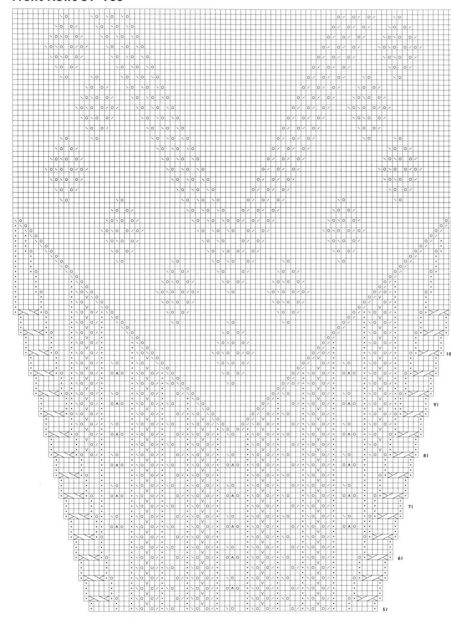

k on RS; p on WS

· p on RS; k on WS

ℓ k1tbl on RS; p1tbl on WS

O yo

╱ k2tog on RS; p2tog on WS

╲ ssk on RS; ssp on WS

λ sl 1 st kwise, k2tog, psso

∧ centered double dec

V sl 1

■ bobble

▨ no stitch

□ pattern repeat

⟍⟋ sl 2 sts onto cn and hold in back
k2, k2 from cn

⟋⟍ sl 2 sts onto cn and hold in front,
k2, k2 from cn

Front Rows 1–50

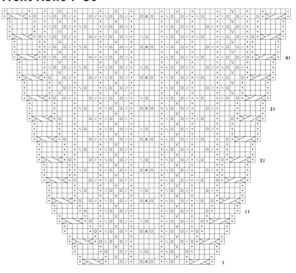

mond patt), ending at garter ridge above bobble band. As for the upper bodice ruffle, these strands are just slipped onto the needle, not picked up and knitted. Make a note of the number of picked-up sts on needle. With dpn, CO 8 sts for ruffle. SET-UP ROW: (WS) K1, p6, purl the last ruffle st tog with first st on cir at left armhole edge—still 8 ruffle sts; 1 picked-up st joined. Work sts on dpn in patt from Large Ruffle chart, and working last st of every WS row as p2tog to join last ruffle st to next picked-up st on cir, rep Rows 1–16 of chart until all picked-up sts have been joined. NOTE: If the original number of picked-up sts on the cir was not a multiple of 8 sts + 1, "fudge" the joining rate as for the upper bodice ruffle by occasionally omitting a p2tog join. When all picked-up sts have been joined, BO ruffle sts.

right ruffle

With RS of front facing and beg at garter ridge above bobble band, use cir needle to pick up 1 strand from every row along the line of purl sts dividing end of front chart from body diamond patt at right front (the purl sts between the cable and the diamond patt), ending at the right armhole edge; these sts are just picked up, not picked up and knitted. Make a note of the number of picked-up sts on needle. With dpn, CO 8 sts for ruffle. SET-UP ROW: (WS) K1, p6, purl the last ruffle st tog with first st on cir at bottom of right front—still 8 ruffle sts; 1 picked-up st joined. Complete as for left ruffle, ending at right armhole edge.

sleeve ruffles

With RS of sleeve facing, use cir needle to pick up the garter st "bump" from each st in the garter ridge just above the lace insert patt; these sts are just picked up, not picked up and knitted. Make a note of the number of picked-up sts on needle. With dpn, CO 8 sts for ruffle. SET-UP ROW: (WS) K1, p6, purl the last ruffle st tog with first st on cir at beg of sleeve RS row— still 8 ruffle sts; 1 picked-up st joined. Work Small Ruffle chart as for upper bodice ruffle, fudging the join as needed. With RS of sleeve facing, use cir needle to pick up the garter st "bump" from each st in the garter ridge just above the zigzag patt, and work a second sleeve ruffle the same as the first. Work 2 ruffles on other sleeve in the same manner.

blocking

This garment must be firmly blocked before assembly. Weave in loose ends. Soak pieces in warm soapy water for 30–60 minutes; do not agitate. Drain and refill the container with clear rinse water. Cont to drain and rinse without agitation until rinse water runs clear. Gently squeeze excess water

out of each piece from top to bottom; do not wring or roll in a towel. Pin each piece to measurements, right side up on a waterproof surface. For the back, overlap the seed st bands and temporarily pin them closed along the length of the back opening. Pin the front and back along the upper shoulders and neck shaping, then stretch pieces down the center to full length. Pin body pieces to full width at the bust, waist and bobble band, pinning bobble band straight across. Place one pin in deepest point of each bear claw at lower edge of body and pull down gently; the bear claw pattern should be allowed to ruffle gently and is not blocked flat. Pulling pieces flat, straight, and smooth, place pins about 1" (2.5 cm) apart around all body edges. Stretch each sleeve from top to bottom to full length and pin the centers of the CO and BO edges. Pin sleeves to full width at cuff, beg of sleeve shaping, end of sleeve shaping, start of cap shaping, and top of sleeve cap. Pulling pieces flat, straight, and smooth, place pins about 1" (2.5 cm) apart around all sleeve edges. Allow all pieces to air-dry completely. NOTE: If the pieces appear to "draw in" after wet-blocking, they may be re-blocked using a thoroughly filled steam iron set to high heat. Place each piece wrong side up on a steam-proof surface, pull gently into shape, and steam. Allow pieces to remain undisturbed until thoroughly dry.

assembly

With yarn threaded on a tapestry needle, sew front to back at shoulders. Sew sleeve caps into armholes, catching both ends of upper bodice ruffle and top ends of lower bodice ruffles in seams, and easing in extra sleeve fullness at top of armhole to create a puffed sleeve effect. Sew sleeve and side seams, leaving CO and BO ends of sleeve ruffles free. Sew CO and BO edges of each sleeve ruffle tog so each ruffle runs continuously around the sleeve. Tack bottom corners of lower bodice ruffles to garter ridge above bobble band. NOTE: The chain selvedges and BO edges form the edging of the neck opening; there is no additional neck finishing. Sew buttons to buttonband of right back, opposite buttonholes.

To prevent stretching, store garment folded; not on a hanger.

design workshop #3

CREATIVE SWATCHING AND SKETCHING

NOW IT'S TIME TO TRANSLATE YOUR MOOD BOARD and color palette into knitting. In this workshop, you'll make a series of swatches and sketches that capture the feelings in your mood board. This part is fun—bringing your idea to life.

Although a gauge swatch is crucial before you begin any project, at this point, we're interested in a different kind of swatch—a "creative swatch." This swatch lets you test your ideas without

investing in a full-size garment. Gather together several yarns that represent the palette you devised in Design Workshop #2 (page 68). If you used paint chips or bits of embroidery thread to fill out your palette, now's the time to find yarns in the same colors. Sort through your yarn stash, pick up odd balls from the sale bin at your yarn shop, and meet with your knitting friends for a "swatching swap." When you have a good representation of the colors in your board, look at them critically to identify ones that work together. You may need to remove some colors or add others to get a workable mixture. Don't worry if the yarns represent a variety of weights or fiber contents—at the moment, only the colors are important.

KNITTING TECHNIQUES

Next, consider ways that the images or objects on your board might be interpreted in knitting. Here's your chance to think like a knitwear designer. Patterns that repeat could be worked into a Fair Isle design. Clear blocks of color, perhaps florals or geometrics, could translate into intarsia. Bold textures might be interpreted in cables or other stitch patterns. Fine or delicate motifs might translate to lace. You get the idea.

STITCH PATTERNS

Look through books of stitch patterns to find ones that capture your mood. Try out a variety of stitches and techniques. Your swatches don't have to match any particular gauge, but it's a good idea to knit the yarns at or near the gauges suggested by the ball bands and to combine yarns of similar weights in color-work swatches. Knit your swatches at least 6 inches (15 centimeters) square so that you can see how the pattern repeats interact horizontally and vertically and so that you can get a good feel for the drape of the fabric. You may want to re-swatch a pattern on larger or smaller needles or substitute one color for another. The goal here is to come up with four or five swatches that reflect the flavor of your mood board. Try to knit at least one each of color work (Fair Isle or intarsia), lace, and textured or cabled patterns. The swatches shown here are some of those that I developed for my beach theme mood board.

CREATIVE COMBINATIONS

Next, consider mixing some of these elements in unexpected ways. Ask yourself "What if?" What if you combine a fine-gauge lace edging with a chunky cable? What if you follow a Fair Isle border with a lacy pattern? What if you knit a thin yarn on big needles? Try knitting two different yarns together for marled effects. This is your chance to be really creative and break out of your comfort zone! You can include all sorts of elements in the same swatch, or you can make separate swatches that can be moved around to see how they work with each other. Assemble the swatches into a collage to see if something appealing but completely different from your initial idea takes shape. Some of my best designs are "happy mistakes" that evolved as I knitted swatches. Feel free to add embellishments: Crochet, embroidery, beads, and felting can all add interest and mood to your pieces.

SILHOUETTE

Finally, you need to think about the basic shape, or silhouette, of the garment you want to make. If you don't have a particular silhouette in mind, look through knitting books and knitting or fashion magazines for ideas. Sketch a potential silhouette and draw the design elements right on top of it. If you have trouble drawing freehand, trace a photograph of a model in a magazine for a foundation.

Sketch in all aspects of your garment. What length will it be? Do you want it to fit loosely or tightly? Will it have waist shaping? What will the neckline look like? Do you want long or short sleeves or something in between? Will the sleeves be fitted or flared? Set-in or raglan? Make a sketch of every combination that interests you—you'll likely end up with lots of good possibilities. Next, sketch in the general look of the stitch textures and other details that you experimented with in your swatches. Don't sketch in every stitch, but include enough to give the impression of how the elements will work together.

FINISHED SIZE

33½ (37½, 41½, 45½, 49½)" (85 [95, 105.5, 115.5, 125.5] cm) bust circumference. Top shown measures 37½" (95 cm). NOTE: The ribbed upper section of this garment molds to the wearer's curves to provide a close, body-conscious fit.

YARN

Fingering weight (#1 Super Fine).

SHOWN HERE: Adrienne Vittadini Celia (100% silk; 109 yd [100 m]/25 g): #001 cream (MC), 6 (7, 8, 9, 10) balls.

DMC Baroque Crochet Cotton Size 10 (100% cotton; 400 yd [365 m]/about 1½ oz): ecru (CC), 1 (1, 2, 2, 2) skein(s).

NEEDLES

Body—size 5 (3.75 mm): straight. Edging—size 2 (3 mm): straight and 32" (80 cm) circular (cir). Adjust needle size if necessary to obtain the correct gauge.

NOTIONS

Stitch holder; removable markers or waste yarn; tapestry needle.

GAUGE

24 stitches and 33½ rows = 4" (10 cm) in butterfly pattern using MC and larger needles; 24 stitches and 36 rows = 4" (10 cm) in k3, p3 rib using either MC or CC and larger needles, with rib stretched so knit and purl columns appear the same width.

{ designer notes }

I've once again used my favorite crochet cotton for the top's fine lace accents. This time, I've paired it with a lovely silk tape yarn. The tape yarn's elasticity provides a comfortable fit, while the inelastic fine cotton allows for greater detail in the lace stitches. I like the subtle color interest that the contrast between the ivory silk and the tea-stained lace provides.

vintage lingerie
TOP

I have a collection of design booklets from the mid to late 1800s and early 1900s that include an assortment of amazing handknitted undergarments, none of which features elastic! Recent fashion trends have moved vintage lingerie, corsets, and other undergarments to the forefront—to be worn as outer garments. This top is my contribution to the current fashion trend of covering modern-day bras with heirloom lingerie.

{ make it your own }

This top would also look quite nice as a sleeveless tank. If you decide to omit the sleeves, you can trim the armholes with a row or two of crochet, worked in either of the two yarns.

stitch guide

BUTTERFLY PATTERN
(MULTIPLE OF 12 STS + 1)

ROW 1: (RS) Knit.

ROW 2: (WS) Purl.

ROW 3: K5, *sl next 3 sts as if to purl with yarn in front (pwise wyf), k9; rep from * to last 8 sts, sl 3 sts pwise wyf, k5.

ROW 4: P5, sl 3 sts pwise with yarn in back (wyb), *p9, sl 3 sts pwise wyb; rep from * to last 5 sts, p5.

ROW 5: K6, *insert tip of right needle underneath both strands of the slip-stitch floats and lift them onto the left needle, knit the next st tog with the lifted strands, k11; rep from * to last 7 sts, insert tip of right needle underneath both strands of the slip-stitch floats and lift them onto the left needle, knit the next st tog with the lifted strands, k6.

ROW 6: P6, *k1, p11; rep from * to last 7 sts, k1, p6.

ROWS 7, 9, AND 15: Knit

ROWS 8 AND 10: Purl.

ROW 11: K6, *k5, sl 3 sts pwise wyf, k4; rep from * to last 7 sts, k7.

ROW 12: P7, *p4, sl 3 sts pwise wyb, p5; rep from * to last 6 sts, p6.

ROW 13: K6, *k6, insert tip of right needle underneath both strands of the slip-stitch floats and lift them onto the left needle, knit the next st tog with the lifted strands, k5; rep from * to last 7 sts, k7.

ROW 14: P12, *k1, p11; rep from * to last 13 sts, k1, p12.

ROW 16: Purl.

Repeat Rows 1–16 for pattern. (Tip: Each st that is knitted tog with the lifted strands on Rows 5 and 13 should be the center st of the 3 slipped sts.)

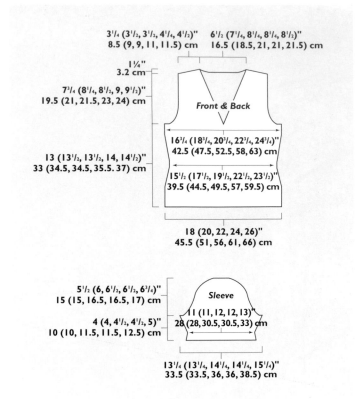

BACK

With CC and larger needles, CO 109 (121, 133, 145, 157) sts. Work Rows 1–12 of Edging chart—piece measures about 1¼" (3.2 cm) at deepest point. (NOTE: Measure all foll lower body lengths from deepest point of edging CO.) Change to MC and work Rows 1–16 of butterfly patt (see Stitch Guide). DEC ROW: (RS) K1, k2tog, work in patt to last 3 sts, ssk, k1—2 sts dec'd. Work 3 rows even. Cont in established patt, rep the shaping of the last 4 rows 6 more times, then work dec row once more—93 (105, 117, 129, 141) sts rem. Work 7 rows even in patt, ending with a WS row—piece measures about 7½" (19 cm) from CO. INC ROW: (RS) K1, M1 (see Glossary), work in patt to last st, M1, k1—2 sts inc'd. Work 3 rows even. Cont in established patt, rep the shaping of the last 4 rows 2 more times, then work inc row once more—101 (113, 125, 137, 149) sts; piece measures about 9" (23 cm) from CO. Work even in patt until piece measures about 10¾" (27.5 cm) from CO, ending with Row 8 or 16 of butterfly patt. Change to CC and smaller straight needles. Work Rows 1–10

Lace Insert

•		•		•		•		•		•	•		•		•		•	•	•		•		•		•	9
								•		•								•	•							
＼	O		O	／		•		•	＼	O		O	／		•		•	＼	O		O	／			7
							•		•						•		•								5
＼	O		O	／		•		•	＼	O		O	／		•		•	＼	O		O	／			5
								•		•								•	•							
＼	O		O	／		•		•	＼	O		O	／		•		•	＼	O		O	／			3
																										1

Edging

•		•		•	O	∧	O	•		•		11
•		•		•		•		•		•		
•		•	O		∧		O	•		•		9
•		•		•		•		•		•		
•		O		∧			O	•		•		7
•		•		•		•		•		•		
•	O			∧				O	•		•	5
•		•		•		•		•		•		
O				∧					O			3
												1

Sleeve

•							•	•		
•							•		•	19
•	•							•	•	
•	•		＼	O				•	•	17
•	•							•	•	15
•	•		＼	O				•	•	13
•	•							•	•	11
•	•		＼	O				•	•	9
•	•							•	•	7
•	•			∧				•	•	5
•	•			∧				•	•	3
•									•	1

of Lace Insert chart. Change to MC and larger needles. Establish rib patt on next row as foll: (RS) P1, *k3, p3; rep from * to last 4 sts, k3, p1. Cont in established rib until piece measures 13 (13½, 13½, 14, 14½)" (33 [34.5, 34.5, 35.5, 37] cm), ending with a WS row.

shape armholes

BO 4 (4, 5, 5, 6) sts at beg of next 2 rows—93 (105, 115, 127, 137) sts rem. Dec 1 st each end of needle every RS row 4 (5, 7, 10, 12) times—85 (95, 101, 107, 113) sts rem. Dec 1 st each end of needle every 4th row 3 (5, 5, 4, 4) times—79 (85, 91, 99, 105) sts rem. Cont even until armholes measures 7¾ (8¼, 8½, 9, 9½)" (19.5 [21, 21.5, 23, 23.5] cm), ending with a WS row.

Legend:

Symbol	Meaning
(blank)	k on **RS**; p on **WS**
•	p on **RS**; k on **WS**
O	yo
／	k2tog
＼	ssk
∧	sl 2 as if to k2tog, k1, p2sso
(shaded)	no stitch
(outlined)	pattern repeat

shape neck and shoulders

(RS) Work 29 (31, 32, 36, 38) sts in patt, place center 21 (23, 27, 27, 29) sts on holder, join new ball of yarn and work in patt to end—29 (31, 32, 36, 38) sts at each side. NOTE: The neck and shoulders are shaped at the same time; read all the way through the foll section before proceeding. Working each side separately, at each neck edge BO 6 (7, 8, 8, 8) sts once, then BO 3 sts once and *at the same time*, at each armhole edge, BO 4 (4, 4, 5, 5) sts 4 times, then BO 4 (5, 5, 5, 7) sts once—no sts rem.

FRONT

CO and work as for back until piece measures 13 (13½, 13½ 14, 14½)" (33 [34.5, 34.5, 35.5, 37] cm), ending with a WS row—101 (113, 125, 137, 149) sts.

shape armholes and neck

Mark center 3 sts with removable markers or waste yarn—49 (55, 61, 67, 73) sts on each side of 3 marked sts. NEXT ROW: (RS) BO 4 (4, 5, 5, 6) sts, work in patt to marked center sts, join new yarn and BO center 3 sts, work in patt to end. NEXT ROW: (WS) Working each side separately, BO 4 (4, 5, 5, 6) sts at beg of first group of sts, then work even to end of second group of sts—45 (51, 56, 62, 67) sts rem at each side. NOTE: Armholes and neck are shaped at the same time; read all the way through the foll section before proceeding. Cont to shape armholes as for back by dec 1 st at armhole edge every other row 4 (5, 7, 10, 12) times, then dec 1 st at armhole edge every 4th row 3 (5, 5, 4, 4) times—7 (10, 12, 14, 16) more sts removed at each side by armhole shaping. *At the same time* dec 1 st at each neck edge every RS row 6 (8, 12, 11, 12) times, then every 4th row 12 (12, 11, 12, 12) times—20 (21, 21, 25, 27) sts rem each side when all armhole and neck shaping is completed. Cont even until armholes measure 7¾ (8¼, 8½, 9, 9½)" (19.5 [21, 21.5, 23, 23.5] cm), ending with a WS row.

shape shoulders

At each armhole edge, BO 4 (4, 4, 5, 5) sts 4 times, then BO 4 (5, 5, 5, 7) sts once—no sts rem.

SLEEVES (MAKE 2)

With CC and smaller straight needles, CO 111 (111, 121, 121, 131) sts. Purl 1 WS row, then work 4 rows even in St st (knit RS rows; purl WS rows). Work Rows 1–10 of Sleeve chart—67 (67, 73, 73, 79) sts rem after completing Row 5.

Change to larger needles. Work Rows 11–20 of chart once, then rep only Rows 19 and 20 to end. *At the same time*, beg on Row 11 of chart, inc 1 st at each end of needle every 4th row 6 times, working new sts into k3, p3 rib—79 (79, 85, 85, 91) sts. Cont even in patt until piece measures 4 (4, 4½, 4½, 5)" (10 [10, 11.5, 11.5, 12.5] cm) from CO with lower edge unrolled, ending with a WS row.

shape cap

BO 4 (4, 5, 5, 6) sts at beg of next 2 rows—71 (71, 75, 75, 79) sts rem. Dec 1 st each end of needle every RS row 3 (3, 5, 5, 7) times, then every 4th row 5 (7, 7, 7, 7) times, then every RS row 6 (4, 4, 4, 4) times—43 sts rem for all sizes. BO 2 sts at beg of next 4 rows, then BO 3 sts at beg of foll 4 rows, then BO 4 sts at beg of foll 2 rows—15 sts rem. BO all sts.

FINISHING

neck trim

With MC threaded on a tapestry needle, sew front to back at shoulders. With CC, cir needle, RS facing, and starting at the beg at the first of 3 BO sts at center front, pick up and knit 51 (54, 55, 58, 62) sts along right front neck edge, 8 sts along shaped right back neck, k21 (23, 27, 27, 29) held back neck sts from holder while dec 1 (0, 0, 0, 1) st at center, pick up and knit 8 sts along shaped left back neck, and 51 (54, 55, 58, 62) sts along left front neck, ending at the last of the 3 BO sts at center front—138 (147, 153, 159, 168) sts total; ends of trim overlap by 3 sts at center front. Do not join for working in the rnd. Working back and forth in rows, knit 2 rows. NEXT ROW: With WS facing, work picot BO as foll: *BO 3 sts, [return st on right needle to left needle and knit it] 3 times for picot chain; rep from *, BO last 3 sts.

Sew sleeves into armholes, matching centers of sleeves with shoulder seams. Sew sleeve and side seams. Sew down small overlap that is created at center front neck. Lightly steam-block MC sections of body. Block CC sections of body and sleeves using an iron and damp pressing cloth. Weave in loose ends.

summer

In summer, we want to slow down, relax, and take pleasure in this long-awaited season of respite. Yet we also try hard to enjoy every moment of sunlight and outdoor fun in the all-too-short weeks between the end of one school year and the beginning of the next. It's a time for weddings, reunions, and vacations. Not surprisingly, knitting tends to slip closer to the bottom of our to-do lists as other activities take over. For the most part, my summer designs are simple enough to work on at the beach or a baseball game. This is the time I reach for shimmery handdyed silk, nubby raw silk, natural linen, and lightweight summery cotton yarns in crisp colors.

In *June,* field grasses inspire a ribbed texture and tiny spiraling periwinkle shells look like bobbles against a rib. The grains of sand become simple seed stitches with a touch of Lurex to mimic a glistening wet beach, and a leaf suggests the texture for a casual summer sweater. Of course, June is the traditional month for weddings—how about a handknitted wedding dress made from fine, bleached cotton?

Carefree *July* days inspire palettes of refreshing shades of blue and white. Clouds in a summer sky, white sails against dark blue Maine waters, bowls of ripe blueberries, steamed red lobsters, and wild raspberries make me think that July is about red, white, and blue! Living near one of the most beautiful harbors in the world, I can't help but include nautical themes in my summer designs. Stripes and ribs in crisp cottons suit this easygoing time of the year.

The bounty of summer culminates in *August,* with color palettes of warm neutrals. Beachcombing excursions garner bowls brimming with this season's collection of beach treasures—dried sea urchins, special pebbles, shells, and sea-glass jewels. They spill over onto our cottage's tables and offer countless ideas for Fair Isle color combinations and simple textured designs. As the end of summer approaches, fields are tall with golden grasses, yellow black-eyed Susans, and swaths of other wildflowers. Monarch butterflies are everywhere, busily tending my garden and getting ready to migrate southward. Their bright wings outlined in deep brown give me an idea for a sweater that has the same effect. The brilliant harvest moon and the glorious pink and peach sunsets make my knitting palette glow in response.

FINISHED SIZE

28 (31½, 35, 38½, 42)" (71 [80, 89, 98, 106.5] cm) bust circumference. Camisole shown measures 28" (71 cm). NOTE: This garment is styled with no wearing ease for a snug, close-to-the-body fit.

YARN

Fingering weight (#1 Super Fine).

SHOWN HERE: K1C2 Ambrosia (70% alpaca, 20% silk, 10% cashmere; 137 yd (125 m)/50 g): #918 fog (light blue), 7 (8, 9, 10, 11) balls.

NEEDLES

Sizes 1 and 2 (2.25 and 2.75 mm): 24" (60 cm) circular (cir). Adjust needle size if necessary to obtain the correct gauge.

NOTIONS

Marker (m); removable markers or safety pins; cable needle (cn); stitch holders; tapestry needle.

GAUGE

28 stitches and 37 rounds = 4" (10 cm) in rib pattern using larger needle; 48 stitches (three 16-stitch pattern repeats) and 44 rounds = 5¼" (13.5 cm) wide and 4" (10 cm) high in cable pattern from chart using smaller needle, after blocking.

{ designer notes }

This camisole's versatile style lets you dress it up or down depending on the yarn you choose. I used a luscious silk-alpaca blend that's appropriate as a strappy top for day or evening wear all year or as a dressy top for the holidays. Believe it or not, if you omit the straps, it can be worn as a curve-hugging skirt! Turn it into a sexy little evening dress by knitting the tube part longer to reach the desired length.

tiny twists
CAMISOLE

The beauty of this minimal camisole lies in its pattern of tiny twisted cables, which resembles woven netting. Although the pattern looks complex, it's quite simple to knit. I was particularly drawn to the intricacy of a small gauge and tiny twists. By careful engineering, I could extend the cables into the straps to give the top a seamless finish.

{ make it your own }

To maintain the continuity of the cables around the bodice, the finished sizes of this top are based on the number of stitches in a full repeat of the cable pattern. If you want more flexibility in the finished size, use needles one size smaller or larger.

stitch guide

RIB PATTERN (MULTIPLE OF 15 STS)

ALL RNDS: *K7, p1, k7; rep from * to end.

Repeat this round for pattern.

RIGHT TWIST (RT; WORKED OVER 2 STS)

Knit second st on left needle but do not slip off, then knit first st on left needle, then slip both sts off left needle tog.

RIGHT CABLE (RC; WORKED OVER 6 STS)

Sl 4 sts onto cn and hold in back of work, k2, knit last 2 sts on cn, then knit first 2 sts on cn.

LEFT CABLE (LC; WORKED OVER 6 STS)

Sl 2 sts onto cn and hold in front of work, k2, knit last 2 sts on cn, then knit first 2 sts on cn. To work LC at beg of rnd as shown on Rnds 13 and 33 of Cable chart, end the previous rnd (Rnd 12 or 32) 2 sts before end-of-rnd marker (m). Work LC over 2 unworked sts from end rnd and first 4 sts of new rnd as foll: Sl 2 sts onto cn and hold in front, remove end-of-rnd m, k2, replace m, knit last 2 sts on cn, then knit first 2 sts on cn, work in patt to last 2 sts of rnd, end k2.

LOWER BODY

With larger needle and using the long-tail method (see Glossary), CO 304 (342, 380, 418, 456) sts. Place marker (pm) and join for working in rnds, being careful not to twist sts. Purl 1 rnd. Work fluted lower edging as foll:

RNDS 1 AND 2: *K7, p5, k7; rep from * to end.

RND 3: *K6, sl 1 as if to purl with yarn in back (pwise wyb), p5, sl 1 pwise wyb, k6; rep from * to end.

RND 4: *K7, p1, p3tog, p1, k7; rep from * to end—272 (306, 340, 374, 408) sts rem.

RNDS 5 AND 7: *K6, sl 1 pwise wyb, p3, sl 1 pwise wyb, k6; rep from * to end.

RNDS 6 AND 8: *K7, p3, k7; rep from * to end.

RND 9: *K6, sl 1 pwise wyb, p3tog, sl 1 pwise wyb, k6; rep from * to end—240 (270, 300, 330, 360) sts rem.

RND 10: *K7, p1, k7; rep from * to end.

RND 11: *K6, sl 1 pwise wyb, p1, sl 1 pwise wyb, k6; rep from * to end.

RND 12: Rep Rnd 10—piece measures about 1¼" (3.2 cm) from CO.

Change to rib patt (see Stitch Guide), and work even in patt until piece measures 14½ (15, 15½, 16, 16)" (37 [38, 39.5, 40.5, 40.5] cm) from CO.

CABLED BODICE

NEXT RND: *K7, p1, M1 (see Glossary), k7; rep from *, ending last rep with k6 to end 1 st before end of rnd marker (m)—256 (288, 320, 352, 384) sts. Temporarily sl last st to right needle, remove m, return slipped st to left needle, replace m—end of rnd m has moved 1 st to the right. Change to smaller needle. Work Rnds 1–12 of Cable chart (page 122) once, rep Rnds 13–32 two times, then work Rnds 33–45 once. Work Rnd 46 of chart, placing a removable marker or safety pin directly in the fabric (not on the needle) after St 1 and St 129 (145, 161, 177, 193) to mark side "seams"; each marker should be in the center of a 2-st right-twist column—128 (144, 160, 176, 192) sts each in 2 marked sections; 66 chart rnds total; piece measures about 20½ (21, 21½, 22, 22)" (52 [53.5, 54.5, 56, 56] cm) from CO and 6" (15 cm) from beg of cable patt for all sizes. BO all sts, leaving side seam markers in place.

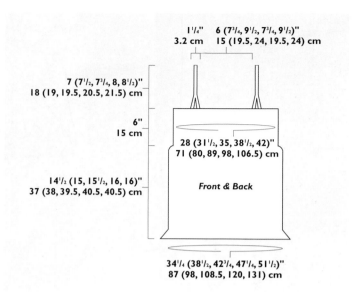

	1¼" 3.2 cm	6 (7¾, 9½, 7¾, 9½)" 15 (19.5, 24, 19.5, 24) cm

7 (7½, 7¾, 8, 8½)"
18 (19, 19.5, 20.5, 21.5) cm

6"
15 cm

28 (31½, 35, 38½, 42)"
71 (80, 89, 98, 106.5) cm

Front & Back

14½ (15, 15½, 16, 16)"
37 (38, 39.5, 40.5, 40.5) cm

34¼ (38½, 42¾, 47¼, 51½)"
87 (98, 108.5, 120, 131) cm

STRAPS

left strap

Lay garment on flat surface with front facing up and side seam markers aligned with the folds at each side. Counting inwards from the side seam marker on your right (the wearer's left), count 26 (26, 26, 42, 42) sts along the BO row, then join yarn to St 27 (27, 27, 43, 43). With smaller needle, pick up and knit St 27 (27, 27, 43, 43) and the next 3 sts after it—4 sts on needle; middle 2 picked-up sts should be directly over a k2 column. NEXT ROW: (WS) K1, p2, k1. Work sts as they appear (knit the knits and purl the purls) for 13 more rows, ending with a RS row—strap measures about 2" (5 cm) from pick-up row. Cut yarn and place sts on holder. Counting inwards from edge of strap just worked, skip the next 4 sts of BO row, and rejoin yarn to next st, St 35 (35, 35, 51, 51) counting from the side marker. With smaller needle, pick up and knit St 35 (35, 35, 51, 51) and the next 3 sts after it—4 sts on needle; middle 2 picked-up sts should be directly over a k2 column. Work 14 rows as for first part of strap, but do not cut yarn. JOINING ROW: (WS) *K1, p2, k1; return 4 held sts for first part of strap to needle and rep from * once more—8 sts. Work cable patt for center of strap as foll:

ROW 1: (RS) P1, LC (see Stitch Guide), p1.

ROWS 2 AND 4: K1, p6, k1.

ROWS 3 AND 5: P1, k6, p1.

ROW 6: Rep Row 2.

Cable

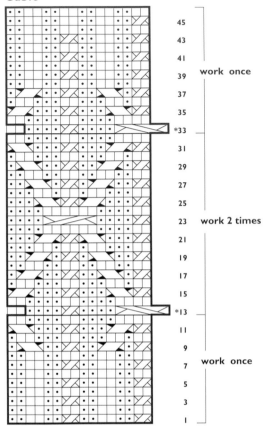

45
43
41
39 work once
37
35
*33
31
29
27
25
23 work 2 times
21
19
17
15
*13
11
9
7 work once
5
3
1

*see Stitch Guide for working Rounds 13 and 33

☐ knit

· purl

☐ pattern repeat

⟩⟨ RT (see Stitch Guide)

sl 1 st onto cn and hold in back,
k2, p1 from cn

sl 2 sts onto cn and hold in front
p1, k2 from cn

RC (see Stitch Guide)

LC (see Stitch Guide)

Rep the last 6 rows until strap measures about 12 (13, 13½, 14, 15)" (30.5 [33, 34.5, 35.5, 38] cm) from BO edge of bodice, or about 2" (5 cm) less than desired strap length, ending with RS Row 3. DIVIDING ROW: (WS) *K1, p2, k1, join new yarn and rep from * once more—2 groups of 4 sts on needle. NEXT ROW: (RS) Working each group separately, work each set of 4 sts as p1, k2, p1. Working each side separately, work sts as they appear for 13 more rows, ending with a WS row. Place sts on holder, but do not cut yarns. Turn garment over with back side facing up and side seam markers still aligned with folds at each side; strap in progress will be on your left, attached to the bottom layer. Counting inwards from the side seam marker on your left (also the wearer's left), count 26 (26, 26, 42, 42) sts along the BO row, then mark St 27 (27, 27, 43, 43) and the next 3 sts after it. Counting inwards from the 4 sts just marked, skip the next 4 sts of BO row, and mark St 35 (35, 35, 51, 51) and the next 3 sts after it—2 marked groups of 4 sts each, middle 2 sts of each group should be directly over a k2 column. Temporarily pin live sts of each strap section to a marked 4-st section, being careful not to twist strap, and forming an upside-down Y as for start of strap. Try on garment to check strap length, and add or remove rows at the ends of the strap as neces-

sary to achieve the best fit. Record the number of rows added or removed so you can make the other strap to match. With yarn threaded on a tapestry needle, use the Kitchener st (see Glossary) to graft live sts at ends of strap to marked 4-st sections in BO row of back.

right strap

Lay garment with front facing up and side seam markers aligned with the folds at each side; strap just completed will be on your right (the wearer's left). Counting inwards from the side seam marker on your left (the wearer's right), count 37 (37, 37, 53, 53) sts along the BO row, then join yarn to St 38 (38, 38, 54, 54). With smaller needle, pick up and knit 4 sts from St 38 (38, 38, 54, 54) to St 35 (35, 35, 51, 51)—4 sts on needle; middle 2 picked-up sts should be directly over a k2 column. Work 14 rows as for left strap, cut yarn, and place sts on holder. Counting out toward the side seam from edge of strap just worked, skip the next 4 sts of BO row, and rejoin yarn to next st, St 30 (30, 30, 46, 46) from the side marker. With smaller needle, pick up and knit 4 sts from St 30 (30, 30, 46, 46) to St 27 (27, 27, 43, 43)—4 sts on needle; middle 2 picked-up sts should be directly over a k2 column. Work 14 rows as for first part of strap, but do not cut yarn. Work joining row and cabled section as for left strap until piece measures about 12 (13, 13½, 14, 15)" (30.5 [33, 34.5, 35.5, 38] cm) from BO edge of bodice, or about 2" (5 cm) less than desired strap length, ending with RS Row 3 of strap cable patt. Work dividing row, then work each part of strap separately for same number of rows as for ends of left strap. Turn garment over with back facing up and side seam markers still aligned with folds at each side; strap in progress will be on your right, attached to the bottom layer. Counting inwards from the side seam marker on your right (the wearer's right), mark 2 groups of 4 sts as for left strap. Graft live sts at ends of strap to marked 4-st sections in BO row of back as for left strap.

FINISHING

Lightly steam-block to measurements as needed. Weave in loose ends.

design
workshop #4
STYLING AND FITTING

THE FINAL STEP IN DESIGNING A KNITTED PIECE is to make a working pattern from your swatches and sketches. To do so, you'll apply your specific size requirements to your silhouette to make a schematic, then you'll use a little math (don't worry—it's the easy kind) to translate those sizes into numbers of stitches and rows.

THE SPECS

The first step is to determine what the finished measurements will be. Because you'll shape the pieces as you knit them, you'll need to know these measurements before you cast on your first stitch. Professional designers create a specifications (spec) sheet to detail the crucial measurements for each project. I've provided a copy of my spec sheet on page 127. Fill in your own body measurements (being sure

to add an allowance for ease) or take measurements from a garment that fits the way you like by laying it flat on a table and measuring the body, sleeve, and neck widths and the body, armhole, and sleeve lengths.

THE SCHEMATIC

The next step is to generate a schematic— a bird's-eye view of all the garment pieces drawn to scale on graph paper. To make a schematic, you'll need graph paper, a pencil, and your spec sheet.

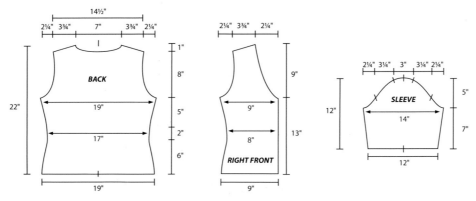

Schematic for a short-sleeved V-neck cardigan.

Start with the schematic for the garment back. First, mark a small vertical centerline as a reference. Make a mark near the bottom of the line, then count up the number of inches (squares) for the overall length and make another mark. Go back to the centerline and count across half the total number of inches (squares) for the width on each side. You have now defined a rectangle that represents the body length and chest width. The armholes, neck, and shoulder slope will be carved from this rectangle.

To keep track of the specific measurements, draw a vertical line to one side of this rectangle and a horizontal line above the top. Write the measurement in inches next to your reference lines for each section that you carve away. Be sure to note both the horizontal and vertical measurements

for every shaping change you make on the schematic. If you want to add waist shaping, add an extra reference line across the middle of the rectangle at the exact height from the lower edge where the waist shaping should be.

Repeat this process for the garment front and again for the sleeves, always referring to the measurements you recorded on your spec sheet for guidance. Draw additional pieces such as collars and pockets separately.

STITCH AND ROW COUNTS

Now it's time to turn your ideas into an annotated schematic for your garment. First, you need to knit an accurate gauge swatch with the yarn and needles you plan to use for your garment so you'll know exactly how many stitches and rows it takes to make one inch of knitted

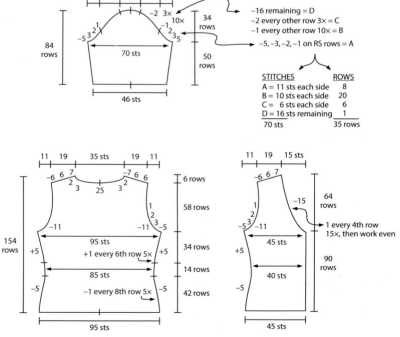

Stitch schematic based on a gauge of 5 stitches and 7 rows per inch.

fabric. The next part involves a bit of math, but don't despair—it's really quite simple if you have a calculator.

Note your stitch gauge (the number of stitches and partial stitches in one inch and your row gauge (the number of rows and partial rows in one inch) on your schematic so you can refer to them for your calculations. For a standard sweater that's worked from the bottom up or from the top down, all horizontal measurements translate into numbers of stitches and all vertical measurements translate into numbers of rows. To make the translations, simply multiply the horizontal measurements by your stitch gauge (i.e., 19 inches × 5 stitches/inch = 95 stitches) and multiply the vertical measurements by your row gauge (i.e., 6 inches × 7 rows/inch = 42 rows). I'll outline the basics for you; if you want a more detailed discussion, refer to one of the books listed in the Bibliography (page 157).

Calculate the number of stitches or rows for each segment of your measurement lines. If shaping is involved (such as at the waist), calculate the number of stitches at the narrowest point and subtract it from the number of stitches at the widest point. The difference is the number of stitches that you'll need to decrease. Calculate the number of rows between the narrowest and widest points to find out how many rows you'll have to accomplish those decreases. Keep in mind that for this type of symmetrical shaping, you'll want to work half of the decreases on each side of the garment.

All that's left is to decide exactly where to place the elements you swatched and sketched in Design Workshop #3 (page 108). Mark where they will go on your schematic, calculate the necessary stitches and rows of these elements, and balance any stitch or color patterns on the center of the schematic. You're ready to knit! You can simply refer to your annotated schematic, or you can write instructions for each section as I've done for the projects in this book.

These directions are meant to highlight the elementary concepts needed to create a schematic and basic working pattern. Practice the technique with a simple shape, then branch out into more detailed designs.

Remember that you can create three-dimensional shapes such as tubes for bodies or sleeves by omitting seams and working in rounds. You will base your calculations on the flat schematic, but work both the front and back at the same time.

SPEC SHEET

BODY		MEASUREMENT
Body Length	(high point of shoulder to hem)	
Body Length	(high point of shoulder to waist)	
Body Width	(across chest)	
Body Width	(at waist)	
Body Width	(at hem)	
Rib Height		
Shoulder Width	(armhole to armhole)	
Armhole Depth	(shoulder to armpit)	
Back Neck Width		
Back Neck Drop	(from high point of shoulder)	
Front Neck Drop	(from high point of shoulder)	
SLEEVE		
Sleeve Length	(from center back to cuff edge)	
Sleeve Length	(from top of shoulder to cuff edge)	
Sleeve Length Underarm	(from underarm to cuff edge)	
Sleeve Cuff Width		
Sleeve Cuff Height		
Sleeve Forearm Width	(6" [15 cm] from cuff edge)	
Sleeve Bicep Width	(1" [2.5 cm] below armhole)	
Sleeve Cap Width	(3" [7.5 cm] from top edge)	
COLLAR		
Collar Height/Type	(at center back neck)	
Collar Height	(at front point)	
Collar Length	(point to point)	
BUTTONS		
Placket Width		
Placket Length		
Button Spacing	(_____ buttons about _____" apart)	
POCKET HEIGHT/WIDTH		

Note: All measurements reflect the garment laying flat on table. Fill in the measurements to create a schematic for your own sweater design.

FINISHED SIZE

32 (36, 39, 42, 45)" (81.5 [91.5, 99, 106.5, 114.5] cm) bust circumference. Top shown measures 32" (81.5 cm).

YARN

Sportweight (#2 Fine).

SHOWN HERE: GGH Scarlett (100% mercerized cotton; 122 yd [112]/50 g): #9 red, 5 (6, 7, 7, 8) balls.

NEEDLES

Size 4 (3.5 mm): straight and 32" (80 cm) circular (cir). Adjust needle size if necessary to obtain the correct gauge.

NOTIONS

Marker; removable markers or safety pins; stitch holders; tapestry needle; size B/1 (2.5 mm) crochet hook; 1 ball DMC Size 5 Pearl Cotton (49 yd [45 m]/10 g) in bleached white for decorative neckline tie.

GAUGE

25 stitches and 33 rows = 4" (10 cm) in stockinette stitch; 26 stitches and 32 rows = 4" (10 cm) in k5, p2 rib pattern for lower body, with rib slightly stretched so 2-stitch purl columns appear about 1 stitch wide.

{ designer notes }

This top begins with a small rectangle at the center of the bust and grows outward from there. The bra sections are worked outward on each side and meet in the back; the ribbed body is worked in the round downward from the base of the bra. Because there are no seams, this piece is easy to knit and wear. The white cording at the neckline adds a nautical flair and makes the red jump to life.

ribbed
HALTER

I wanted to design a top that was bright, summery, and easy to knit. I found inspiration for this halter in bits of fishermen's rope, cheerfully striped buoys, and my local annual Lobster Festival. Cotton was the obvious choice for yarn. I like quick and easy projects for the summer—the season is too short for long, involved knitting.

{ make it your own }

Be sure to try on the bra section before joining the back seam and add or subtract rows as necessary for a comfortable fit. Don't be surprised if the upper edge rolls—the crochet edging will pull it in to lie flat. If necessary, work fewer crochet stitches to help tighten it up.

¤ Each half of the bodice begins by picking up stitches along one side of the center front rectangle. The right and left fronts are worked out to the sides and around to center back where the live stitches of the two halves are grafted together.

¤ Stitches for the lower body are picked up around the lower edge of the completed bodice and worked downwards to the bottom edge.

BODICE

center front

With straight needles and using the long-tail method (see Glossary), CO 9 sts. NEXT ROW: (RS) [K1, p1] 4 times, k1. NEXT ROW: (WS) [P1, k1] 4 times, p1. Rep the last 2 rows until piece measures 2½ (2½, 3, 3¼, 3½)" (6.5 [6.5, 7.5, 8.5, 9] cm) from CO, ending with a WS row. BO all sts.

right front

Hold center front rectangle with RS facing and selvedges at top and bottom. With straight needles and RS facing, pick up and knit 16 (16, 19, 21, 22) sts along top selvedge. Purl 1 WS row. INC ROW: (RS) K2, [yo, k1] 6 (6, 7, 7, 8) times, [yo, k2] 4 (4, 5, 6, 6) times—26 (26, 31, 34, 36) sts. Purl 1 WS row.

ROW 1: K1, p1, k1, yo, knit to end—1 st inc'd.

ROW 2: Purl to last 2 sts, k1, p1.

ROW 3: K1, p1, knit to end.

ROW 4: Rep Row 2.

Rep the last 4 rows 9 (11, 12, 13, 14) more times—36 (38, 44, 48, 51) sts. Work Row 1 once more, placing a removable marker or safety pin at beg of row to indicate strap placement—37 (39, 45, 49, 52) sts. Work Rows 2, 3, and 4—piece measures about 5¾ (6¾, 7¼, 7¾, 8¼)" (14.5 [17, 18.5, 19.5, 21] cm) from pick-up row. NEXT ROW: (RS) K1, p1, k1, k2tog, knit to end—1 st dec'd. NEXT ROW: (WS) Purl to last 5 sts, p2tog, p1, k1, p1—1 st dec'd. Rep the last 2 rows 5 (5, 6, 7, 8) more times—25 (27, 31, 33, 34) sts rem. NEXT ROW: (RS) [K1, p1] 2 times, k1, [ssk, k3] 4 (4, 5, 5, 5) times, ssk 0 (1, 0, 1, 1) time, k0 (0, 1, 1, 2)—21 (22, 26, 27, 28) sts rem; piece measures about 7¼ (8¼, 9, 9¾, 10½)" (18.5 [21, 23, 25, 26.5] cm) from pick-up row measured along straight selvedge at end of RS rows; do not measure along shaped selvedge at beg of RS rows. With removable markers or safety pins, mark both ends of last row to indicate side

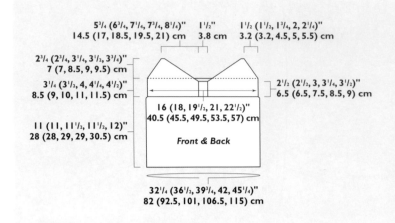

5¾ (6¾, 7¼, 7¾, 8¼)"
14.5 (17, 18.5, 19.5, 21) cm   1½" 3.8 cm   1½ (1½, 1¾, 2, 2¼)" 3.2 (3.2, 4.5, 5, 5.5) cm

2¾ (2¾, 3¼, 3½, 3¾)"
7 (7, 8.5, 9, 9.5) cm

3¼ (3½, 4, 4¼, 4½)"
8.5 (9, 10, 11, 11.5) cm   2½ (2½, 3, 3¼, 3½)"
                                         6.5 (6.5, 7.5, 8.5, 9) cm

16 (18, 19½, 21, 22½)"
40.5 (45.5, 49.5, 53.5, 57) cm

11 (11, 11½, 11½, 12)"
28 (28, 29, 29, 30.5) cm   **Front & Back**

32¼ (36½, 39¾, 42, 45¼)"
82 (92.5, 101, 106.5, 115) cm

"seam." NEXT ROW: (WS) Purl to last 4 sts, [k1, p1] 2 times. NEXT ROW: (RS) [K1, p1] 2 times, knit to end. Rep the last 2 rows until piece measures 8 (9, 9¾, 10½, 11¼)" (20.5 [23, 25, 26.5, 28.5] cm) from side seam markers, ending with a WS row. Place sts on holder.

left front

Hold piece with RS facing, rem selvedge of center front piece at top, and straight selvedge of right front on your right. With straight needles and RS facing, pick up and knit 16 (16, 19, 21, 22) sts along rem selvedge of center front. Purl 1 WS row. INC ROW: (RS) [K2, yo] 4 (4, 5, 6, 6) times, [k1, yo] 6 (6, 7, 7, 8) times, k2—26 (26, 31, 34, 36) sts. Purl 1 WS row.

ROW 1: Knit to last 3 sts, yo, k1, p1, k1—1 st inc'd.

ROW 2: P1, k1, purl to end.

ROW 3: Knit to last 2 sts, p1, k1.

ROW 4: Rep Row 2.

Rep the last 4 rows 10 (12, 13, 14, 15) more times—37 (39, 45, 49, 52) sts; piece measures about 5¾ (6¾, 7¼, 7¾, 8¼)" (14.5 [17, 18.5, 19.5, 21] cm) from pick-up row. Place removable marker at beg of last WS row to indicate strap placement. NEXT ROW: (RS) Knit to last 5 sts, ssk, k1, p1, k1—1 st dec'd. NEXT ROW: (WS) P1, k1, p1, ssp (see Glossary), purl to end—1 st dec'd. Rep the last 2 rows 5 (5, 6, 7, 8) more times—25 (27, 31, 33, 34) sts. NEXT ROW: (RS) K0 (0, 1, 1, 2), k2tog 0 (1, 0, 1, 1) time, [k3, k2tog] 4 (4, 5, 5, 5) times, k1, [p1, k1] 2 times—21 (22, 26, 27, 28) sts rem; piece measures about 7¼ (8¼, 9, 9¾, 10½)" (18.5 [21, 23, 25, 26.5] cm) from pick-up row measured along straight selvedge at beg of RS rows. With removable markers, mark both ends of last row to indicate side "seam." NEXT ROW: (WS) [P1, k1] 2 times, purl to end. NEXT ROW: (RS) Knit to last 4 sts, [p1, k1] 2 times. Rep the last 2 rows until piece measures 8 (9, 9¾, 10½, 11¼)" (20.5 [23, 25, 26.5, 28.5] cm) from side seam markers, ending with a WS row. Place sts on holder.

LOWER BODY

Return held sts of right and left fronts to needle and, with yarn threaded on a tapestry needle, use the Kitchener st (see Glossary) to graft live sts at ends of bodice tog at center back to form a tube, being careful not to twist pieces. Hold assembled bodice upside down with straight selvedge across the top. With cir needle, RS facing, and beg at right side seam marker, pick up and knit 49 (56, 61, 65, 70) sts along lower edge of right front bodice, 7 sts from CO edge of center front piece, 49 (56, 61, 65, 70) sts along lower edge of left front bodice, place regular marker on needle (pm), and pick up and knit 105 (119, 130, 136, 147) sts along lower edge of back—210 (238, 259, 273, 294) sts total. Pm and join for working in rnds. Set-up rib patt on next rnd as foll for your size:

sizes 32 (36, 45)" only

P1, k5, [p2, k5] 6 (7, 9) times, p1, work 7 sts picked up from center front piece as [p1, k5, p1], p1, [k5, p2] 6 (7, 9) times, k5, p1, slip side marker, p1, [k5, p2] 14 (16, 20) times, k5, p1.

size 39" only

K4, [p2, k5] 8 times, p1, work 7 sts picked up from center front piece as [p1, k5, p1], p1, [k5, p2] 8 times, k4, slip side marker, k1, p2, [k5, p2] 18 times, k1.

size 42" only

K1, [p2, k5] 9 times, p1, work 7 sts picked up from center front piece as [p1, k5, p1], p1, [k5, p2] 9 times, k1, slip side marker, k4, p2, [k5, p2] 18 times, k4.

all sizes

Cont even in established k5, p2 rib patt (knit the knits and purl the purls as they appear) until piece measures 11 (11, 11½, 11½, 12)" (28 [28, 29, 29, 30.5] cm from pick-up rnd. BO all sts loosely in rib patt.

FINISHING

straps

With straight needles, RS facing, and beg at strap marker on right front, pick up and knit 5 sts across "peak" of right front shaping. NEXT ROW: (WS) [P1, k1] 2 times, p1. Cont in rib as established until strap measures 25" (63.5 cm) from pick-up row for all sizes or desired length, ending with a WS row. BO all sts in rib patt. Rep for left strap, picking up sts beg at marked position at peak of left front shaping.

drawstrings

With CC and crochet hook (see Glossary for crochet instructions), make a crochet chain about 15 (17, 17½, 20, 21½)" (38 [43, 44.5, 51, 54.5] cm) long. Turn, and work a slip stitch in each ch to end. Fasten off last st. Make a second drawstring the same as the first. Weave drawstrings in and out of eyelet holes along shaped upper edge of bodice, starting by entering the eyelet closest to center front from the RS. With tail threaded on a tapestry needle, anchor one end of each drawstring on WS near base of strap. Tie loose ends of drawstrings tog in a bow at center front.

neck trim

With crochet hook, RS facing, and beg at upper edge of center back, work a row of single crochet across the back, up the left front to base of strap, work 3 sc at top of left peak, cont in sc to base of right strap, work 3 sc at top of right peak, cont in sc to center back, join with a slip stitch. With RS still facing, work a row of rev sc, working 3 sts in center st at top of each peak. Fasten off last st.

Weave in loose ends. Steam-block with iron and damp cloth, being careful not to flatten ribbing in lower body.

FINISHED SIZE

35 (39, 43, 47, 51)" (89 [99, 109, 119.5, 129.5] cm) bust circumference, buttoned. Sweater shown measures 35" (89 cm).

YARN

Sportweight (#2 Fine).

SHOWN HERE: Schoeller Stahl Palma (100% mercerized cotton; 120 yd [110 m]/ 50 g): #25 aqua (MC), 8 (9, 10, 11, 12) balls; #20 espresso (CC), 2 (2, 2, 3, 3) balls.

NEEDLES

Body and sleeves—size 4 (3.5 mm). Waist rib and edging—size 3 (3.25 mm): 32" (80 cm) circular (cir). Adjust needle size if necessary to obtain the correct gauge.

NOTIONS

Markers (m); stitch holder; tapestry needle; crochet hook size B/1 (2.25 mm); nine ½" (1.3 cm) assorted jet glass buttons.

GAUGE

24 stitches and 31 rows = 4" (10 cm) in stockinette stitch using larger needles; 7-stitch front cable patterns measure 1" (2.5 cm) wide.

{ designer notes }

The stitch pattern at the hem of this sweater can be a challenge to knit. The zigzag shape is created by aligned decreases worked on both right- and wrong-side rows. To familiarize your-self with the somewhat tricky pattern, practice several repeats on a swatch before embarking on the full garment.

papillon
CARDIGAN

In late summer, dozens of butterflies visit my garden in a final spree before cool weather hits. Each vibrantly colored wing, patterned with dots and outlined in dark browns, is an individual work of art. For this sweater, I copied the color from an exotic specimen my daughter bought at a museum store—vibrant turquoise outlined with the deepest brown.

{ make it your own }

Look closely at butterflies or other insects in your area and choose your own favorite colors—monarch orange, warm beige, yellowy gold, and seafoam blue worked with dark brown accents would all be beautiful.

stitch guide

CABLE FOR RIGHT FRONT
(WORKED OVER 7 STS)

ROWS 1 AND 5: (RS) K1, p1, k4, p1.

ROWS 2, 4, AND 6: (WS) K1, p4, k1, p1.

ROW 3: K1, p1, sl 2 sts onto cn and hold in front of work, k2, k2 from cn, p1.

ROW 7: K1, p1, sl 2 sts onto cn and hold in back of work, k2, k2 from cn, p1.

ROW 8: Rep Row 2.

Repeat Rows 1–8 for pattern.

CABLE FOR LEFT FRONT
(WORKED OVER 7 STS)

ROWS 1 AND 5: (RS) P1, k4, p1, k1.

ROWS 2, 4, AND 6: (WS) P1, k1, p4, k1.

ROW 3: P1, sl 2 sts onto cn and hold in back of work, k2, k2 from cn, p1, k1.

ROW 7: P1, sl 2 sts onto cn and hold in front of work, k2, k2 from cn, p1, k1.

ROW 8: Rep Row 2.

Repeat Rows 1–8 for pattern.

BOBBLE

Work k1, p1, k1 all in same st—3 sts made from 1 st. Turn, p3, turn, k3, turn, p3, turn, k1, k2tog, psso—3 sts dec'd back to 1 st.

NOTES

¤ The shoulder seams for this garment are offset toward the back, and the back armholes are shorter than the front armholes. Sloped shoulder shaping is worked only on the back, and the front shoulders are bound off straight across.

¤ When sewing in the sleeves, lay the garment flat to find the top of the armhole opening (about ½" to ¾" [2.5 to 4.5 cm] forward of the shoulder seam), and match the center of the sleeve cap to the top of the armhole, not to the shoulder seam.

BACK

With MC, larger needles, and using the long-tail method (see Glossary), CO 105 (117, 129, 141, 153) sts. Purl 1 WS row. SET-UP ROW: (RS) K4 (10, 4, 10, 4), work Row 1 of Lace Border chart (page 136) over center 97 (97, 121, 121, 145) sts, k4 (10, 4, 10, 4). Working sts outside chart patt at each side in St st, work Rows 2–8 of chart, then work Rows 1 and 2 once more. NEXT ROW: (RS, Row 3 of chart) K1, k2tog, work in patt to last 3 sts, ssk, k1—2 sts dec'd. Cont in patt, work Rows 4–8 of chart, then work Rows 1–4 once more. NEXT ROW: (RS, Row 5 of chart) K1, k2tog, work in patt to last 3 sts, ssk, k1—101 (113, 125, 137, 149) sts rem. Work Rows 6–8 of chart—24 chart rows completed; piece measures about 3¼" (8.5 cm) from CO. Change to smaller needles. NEXT ROW: (RS) *K1, p1; rep from * to last st, k1. Work 3 rows even in established rib (knit the knits and purl the purls as they appear), ending with a WS row. EYELET ROW: (RS) *Work 4 sts in rib patt, yo, k2tog; rep from * to last 5 sts, work 5 sts in rib patt—16 (18, 20, 22, 24) eyelet holes completed. Work 5 rows even in rib patt, ending with a WS row—piece measures about 4½" (11.5 cm) from CO. Change to larger needles and St st. Work even until piece measures 9" (23 cm) from CO, ending with a WS row. Inc 1 st at each end of needle on next RS row—2 sts inc'd. Work even for 13 rows, ending with a WS row. Inc 1 st at each end of needle on next RS row—105 (117, 129, 141, 153) sts. Work even until piece measures 13 (13, 13½, 13½, 14)" (33 [33, 34.5, 34.5, 35.5] cm) from CO, ending with a WS row.

shape armholes

BO 5 (6, 7, 8, 9) sts at beg of next 2 rows, then BO 3 (4, 5, 6, 7) sts at beg of foll 2 rows—89 (97, 105, 113, 121) sts rem. DEC ROW: K1, k2tog, knit to last 3 sts, ssk, k1—2 sts dec'd. Dec 1 st each end of needle in the manner on the next 2 (2, 3, 6, 7) RS rows—83 (91, 97, 99, 105) sts rem. Work even until armholes measure 7 (7½, 8, 8½, 9)" (18 [19, 20.5, 21.5, 23] cm), ending with a WS row.

shape neck and shoulders

Mark center 21 (23, 23, 25, 25) sts. BO 3 (3, 4, 4, 4) sts at beg of next 8 rows—59 (67, 65, 67, 73) sts rem. NEXT ROW: (RS) BO 3 (4, 4, 4, 5) sts, knit to marked center sts, place center 21 (23, 23, 25, 25) sts on holder, join new ball of yarn, knit to end. NEXT ROW: (WS) Working each side separately, BO 3 (4, 4, 4, 5) sts at beg of first group of sts, work even across second group of sts—16 (18, 17, 17, 19) sts rem at each side. Working each side separately, at each neck edge BO 5 sts 2 times and *at the same time*, at each armhole edge BO 3 (4, 4, 4, 5) sts once, then BO 3 (4, 3, 3, 4) sts once—no sts rem.

RIGHT FRONT

With MC, larger needles, and using the long-tail method, CO 55 (61, 67, 73, 79) sts. Purl 1 WS row. SET-UP ROW: (RS) K2 (garter edge sts; knit every row) work Row 1 of Lace Border chart over next 49 (49, 61, 61, 73) sts, k4 (10, 4, 10, 4). Working 2 sts at front edge (beg of RS rows, end of WS rows) in garter st and sts at side edge (end of RS rows; beg of WS rows) in St st, work Rows 2–8 of chart, then work Rows 1 and 2 once more. NEXT ROW: (RS; Row 3 of chart) Work in patt to last 3 sts, ssk, k1—1 st dec'd. Cont in patt, work Rows 4–8 of chart, then work Rows 1–4 once more. NEXT ROW: (RS; Row 5 of chart) Work in patt to last 3 sts, ssk, k1—53 (59, 65, 71, 77) sts rem. Work Rows 6–8 of chart—24 chart rows completed; piece measures about 3¼" (8.5 cm) from CO. Change to smaller needles. NEXT ROW: (RS) K2 (edge sts), *p1, k1; rep from * to last 3 sts, p1, k2. Keeping edge sts in garter st, work 3 rows in established rib, ending with a WS

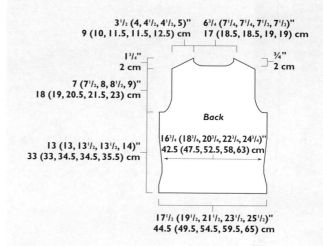

3½ (4, 4½, 4½, 5)"
9 (10, 11.5, 11.5, 12.5) cm

6¾ (7¼, 7¼, 7½, 7½)"
17 (18.5, 18.5, 19, 19) cm

1¾"
2 cm

¾"
2 cm

7 (7½, 8, 8½, 9)"
18 (19, 20.5, 21.5, 23) cm

Back

16¾ (18¾, 20¾, 22¾, 24¾)"
42.5 (47.5, 52.5, 58, 63) cm

13 (13, 13½, 13½, 14)"
33 (33, 34.5, 34.5, 35.5) cm

17½ (19½, 21½, 23½, 25½)"
44.5 (49.5, 54.5, 59.5, 65) cm

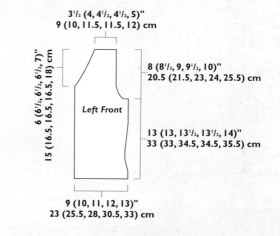

3½ (4, 4½, 4½, 5)"
9 (10, 11.5, 11.5, 12) cm

6 (6½, 6½, 6½, 7)"
15 (16.5, 16.5, 16.5, 18) cm

8 (8½, 9, 9½, 10)"
20.5 (21.5, 23, 24, 25.5) cm

Left Front

13 (13, 13½, 13½, 14)"
33 (33, 34.5, 34.5, 35.5) cm

15 (16.5, 16.5, 16.5, 18) cm

9 (10, 11, 12, 13)"
23 (25.5, 28, 30.5, 33) cm

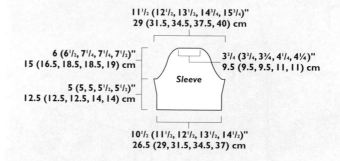

11½ (12½, 13½, 14¾, 15¾)"
29 (31.5, 34.5, 37.5, 40) cm

6 (6½, 7¼, 7¼, 7½)"
15 (16.5, 18.5, 18.5, 19) cm

3¾ (3¾, 3¾, 4¼, 4¼)"
9.5 (9.5, 9.5, 11, 11) cm

Sleeve

5 (5, 5, 5½, 5½)"
12.5 (12.5, 12.5, 14, 14) cm

10½ (11½, 12½, 13½, 14½)"
26.5 (29, 31.5, 34.5, 37) cm

row. EYELET ROW: (RS) K2 (edge sts), p1, yo, k2tog, [work 4 sts in rib patt, yo, k2tog] 7 (8, 9, 10, 11) times, work 6 sts in patt—8 (9, 10, 11, 12) eyelet holes completed. Keeping edge sts in garter st, work 5 rows even in rib patt, ending with a WS row—piece measures about 4½" (11.5 cm) from CO. Change to larger needles. SET-UP ROW: (RS) K2 (edge sts), work cable for right front (see Stitch Guide) over next 7 sts, place marker (pm), work in St st to end. Work in established patt until piece measures 9" (23 cm) from CO, ending with a WS row. Inc 1 st at end of needle on next RS row—1 st inc'd. Work even for 13 rows, ending with a WS row. Inc 1 st at end of needle on next RS row—55 (61, 67, 73, 79) sts. Work even until piece measures 13 (13, 13½, 13½, 14)" (33 [33, 34.5, 34.5, 35.5] cm) from CO, ending with a RS row.

shape armhole

BO 5 (6, 7, 8, 9) sts at beg of next WS row, then BO 3 (4, 5, 6, 7) sts at beg of foll WS row—47 (51, 55, 59, 63) sts rem. DEC ROW: Work in patt to last 3 sts, ssk, k1—1 st dec'd. Dec 1 st at end of needle in this manner on the next 2 (2, 3, 6, 7) RS rows—44 (48, 51, 52, 55) sts rem. Work even until armhole measures 2 (2, 2½, 3, 3)" (5 [5, 6.5, 7.5, 7.5] cm) ending with a WS row.

shape neck

DEC ROW: (RS) Work 9 sts in patt, slip marker (sl m), ssk, knit to end of row—1 st dec'd. Dec 1 st at neck edge in this manner every RS row 22 (23, 23, 24, 24) more times—21 (24, 27, 27, 30) sts rem. Work even in patt until armhole measures 8 (8½, 9, 9½, 10)" (20.5 [21.5, 23, 24, 25.5] cm), ending with a WS row. BO rem sts.

LEFT FRONT

With MC, larger needles, and using the long-tail method, CO 55 (61, 67, 73, 79) sts. Purl 1 WS row. SET-UP ROW: (RS) K4 (10, 4, 10, 4) sts, work Row 1 of Lace Border chart over next 49 (49, 61, 61, 73) sts, k2 (garter edge sts; knit every row). Working 2 sts at front edge (end of RS rows; beg of WS rows) in garter st and working sts at side edge (beg of RS rows; end of WS rows) in St st, work Rows 2–8 of chart, then work Rows 1 and 2 once more. NEXT ROW: (RS; Row 3 of chart) K1, k2tog, work in patt to end—1 st dec'd. Cont in patt, work Rows 4–8 of chart, then work Rows 1–4 once more. NEXT ROW: (RS; Row 5 of chart) K1, k2tog, work in patt to end—53 (59, 65, 71, 77) sts rem. Work Rows 6–8 of chart—24 chart rows completed; piece measures about 3¼" (8.5 cm) from CO. Change to smaller needles. NEXT ROW: (RS) K2, p1, *k1,

k on RS; p on WS

· p on RS; k on WS

○ yo

∕ k2tog on RS; p2tog on WS

∖ ssk on RS; ssp on WS

pattern repeat

Lace Border

p1; rep from * to last 2 sts, k2 (edge sts). Keeping edge sts in garter st, work 3 rows in established rib, ending with a WS row. EYELET ROW: (RS) Work 6 sts in patt, [k2tog, yo, work 4 sts in rib patt] 7 (8, 9, 10, 11) times, k2tog, yo, p1, k2 (edge sts)—8 (9, 10, 11, 12) eyelet holes completed. Keeping edge sts in garter st, work 5 rows even in rib patt, ending with a WS row—piece measures about 4½" (11.5 cm) from CO. Change to larger needles. SET-UP ROW: Work in St st to last 9 sts, pm, work cable for left front (see Stitch Guide) over next 7 sts, k2 (edge sts). Work in established patt until piece measures 9" (23 cm) from CO, ending with a WS row. Inc 1 st at beg of needle on next RS row—1 st inc'd. Work even for 13 rows, ending with a WS row. Inc 1 st at beg of needle on next RS row—55 (61, 67, 73, 79) sts. Work even until piece measures 13 (13, 13½, 13½, 14)" (33 [33, 34.5, 34.5, 35.5] cm) from CO, ending with a WS row.

shape armhole

BO 5 (6, 7, 8, 9) sts at beg of next RS row, then BO 3 (4, 5, 6, 7) sts at beg of foll RS row—47 (51, 55, 59, 63) sts rem. DEC ROW: K1, k2tog, work in patt to end—1 st dec'd. Dec 1 st at beg of needle in this manner on the next 2 (2, 3, 6, 7) RS rows—44 (48, 51, 52, 55) sts rem. Work even until armhole measures 2 (2, 2½, 3, 3)" (5 [5, 6.5, 7.5, 7.5] cm) ending with a WS row.

shape neck

DEC ROW: (RS) Knit to last 11 sts, k2tog, sl m, work in patt to end—1 st dec'd. Dec 1 st at neck edge in this manner every RS row 22 (23, 23, 24, 24) more times—21 (24, 27, 27, 30) sts rem. Work even in patt until armhole measures 8 (8½, 9, 9½, 10)" (20.5 [21.5, 23, 24, 25.5] cm), ending with a WS row. BO rem sts.

SLEEVES (MAKE 2)

With CC, larger needles, and using the long-tail method, CO 63 (69, 75, 81, 87) sts. Purl 1 WS row. SET-UP ROW: (RS) K1 (4, 1, 4, 1) work Row 1 of Lace Border chart over center 61 (61, 73, 73, 85) sts, k1 (4, 1, 4, 1). Working sts outside chart patt at each side in St st, work Rows 2–8 once, then rep Rows 1–8 once more. Change to MC. Knit the next 2 rows for garter ridge, then work 2 rows in St st, ending with a WS row. BOBBLE ROW: (RS) K6 (6, 7, 5, 6) with MC, *make bobble with CC (see Stitch Guide), k4; rep from * to last 2 (3, 3, 1, 1) st(s) carrying CC yarn loosely across the WS to where it is needed for the next bobble, k2 (3, 3, 1, 1) with MC. With MC, purl 1 WS row—piece measures about 2½" (6.5 cm) from CO. Cont in St st with MC, beg on the next RS row inc 1 st

at each end of needle every 4 rows 3 (3, 3, 4, 4) times—69 (75, 81, 89, 95) sts. Work even until piece measures 5 (5, 5, 5½, 5½)" (12.5 [12.5, 12.5, 14, 14] cm) from CO, ending with a WS row.

shape cap

BO 5 (6, 7, 8, 9) sts at beg of next 2 rows, then BO 3 (4, 5, 6, 7) sts at beg of foll 2 rows—53 (55, 57, 61, 63) sts rem. DEC ROW: K1, k2tog, knit to last 3 sts, ssk, k1—2 sts dec'd. Dec 1 st each end of needle in this manner every RS row 6 (7, 9, 8, 9) more times, then every other RS row 6 (7, 9, 8, 9) times—23 (23, 23, 25, 25) sts rem. BO all sts.

FINISHING

Lightly steam-block all pieces to measurements. With MC threaded on a tapestry needle, use the invisible horizontal seam (see Glossary) to sew straight shoulder edges of fronts to shaped shoulder edges of back.

neck trim

Mark position of 9 buttonholes on right front edge, the lowest 2" (5 cm) up from CO edge, the highest at beg of neck shaping, and the rem 7 evenly spaced in between. With CC, smaller cir needle, RS facing, and beg at CO edge of right front, pick up and knit 11 sts to first buttonhole marker, yo, skip next edge st, *pick up and knit 5 (5, 6, 6, 6) sts to next marker, yo, skip next edge st, pick up and knit 5 (5, 5, 6, 6) sts to next marker, yo, skip next edge st; rep from * 3 more times (9 yo buttonholes completed), pick up and knit 29 (31, 31, 31, 33) sts along right front neck to shoulder seam, 8 sts along right back neck shaping, k21 (23, 23, 25, 25) held back neck sts, pick up and knit 8 sts along left back neck shaping, 29 (31, 31, 31, 33) sts along left front neck, and 60 (60, 64, 68, 68) sts to CO edge of left front—215 (221, 229, 239, 243) sts total, including yos. Knit 1 WS row. BO all sts.

belt

With CC and crochet hook, work a crochet chain (see Glossary for crochet instructions) about 66 (70, 74, 78, 82)" (168 [178, 188, 198, 208] cm) long. Work 1 single crochet st into each ch. Fasten off. Beg at right front, weave belt in and out through eyelet holes in ribbed waist section as shown.

With MC threaded on a tapestry needle, sew sleeve caps into armholes, aligning center of each cap with top of armhole and not the shoulder seam (see Notes). Sew sleeve and side seams. Weave in loose ends. Steam-block all seams if desired. Sew buttons to left front opposite buttonholes.

FINISHED SIZE

TOP: 32 (36, 42, 47)" (81.5 [91.5, 106.5, 119.5] cm) bust circumference, buttoned. Top shown measures 36" (91.5 cm).

SKIRT: 36¼ (40, 45½, 49)" (92 [101.5, 115.5, 124.5] cm) hip circumference, and 35" (89 cm) long from deepest point of lower border to bottom of waistband. Skirt shown measures 40" (101.5 cm). Directions are given for adjusting skirt length.

YARN

DK weight (#3 Light), worsted weight (#4 Medium), and fingering weight (#1 Super Fine).

SHOWN HERE: Berroco Cotton Twist (70% cotton, 30% rayon; 85 yd [78 m]/50 g): #8301 bleach white (MC), 6 (7, 8, 10) skeins for top; 4 (4, 5, 6) skeins for skirt.

DMC Baroque Crochet Cotton Size 10 (100% cotton; 400 yd [365 m]/ about 1½ oz: bleach white (A), 1 (1, 1, 2) skein(s) for top; 2 (2, 2, 3) skeins for skirt.

Rowan Cotton Glace (100% cotton; 125 [114 m]/ 50 g): #726 bleached (B; white), 2 (2, 2, 3) skeins for top; 3 (3, 4, 5) skeins for skirt.

Berroco Touche (50% cotton, 50% rayon; 89 yd [81 m]/50 g): #7900 bleach (C; white), 3 (3, 4, 5) skeins for skirt.

NEEDLES

Top body and neck edging—sizes 4 and 7 (3.5 and 4.5 mm): 32" (80 cm) circular (cir). Top sleeves and buttonbands—sizes 3 and 5 (3.25 and 3.75 mm): straight. Skirt—sizes 3, 4, 6, and 7 (3.25, 3.5, 4, and 4.5 mm): 32" (80 cm) cir. Adjust needle size if necessary to obtain the correct gauge.

NOTIONS

Markers (m); stitch holder; tapestry needle; eleven (twelve, twelve, thirteen) ⅜" (1 cm) buttons for top; five ⅜" (1 cm) buttons for skirt; ⅜" (1 cm) waistband elastic for skirt in length to fit comfortably around wearer's waist plus 1" (2.5 cm) overlap; sharp-point sewing needle and matching thread for sewing buttons and waist elastic.

GAUGE

TOP: 22 stitches and 28 rows = 4" (10 cm) in stockinette stitch with MC on larger circular needle; 20 stitches (2 pattern repeats) of Shells chart measure 3¾" (9.5 cm wide) with B on larger circular needle; 39 stitches (3 pattern repeats) and 24 rows (6 pattern repeats) of sleeve pattern measure 5½" (14 cm) wide and 2¼" (5.5 cm) high with A on smaller straight needles, after blocking.

SKIRT: 22 stitches and 28 rows = 4" (10 cm) in stockinette stitch with MC on largest needle; 44 stitches (widest point) and 36 rows (2 repeats) of Border chart measure 7" (18 cm) wide and 5½" (14 cm) high with A on second-largest circular needle after blocking; 18 stitches and 25 rows = 4" (10 cm) in reverse stockinette stitch with C on largest needle; 20 stitches (2 patt repeats) of Shells chart measure 3¾" (9.5 cm) wide with B on largest needle; 24 stitches and 34½ rows = 4" (10 cm) in stockinette stitch with B on smallest needle.

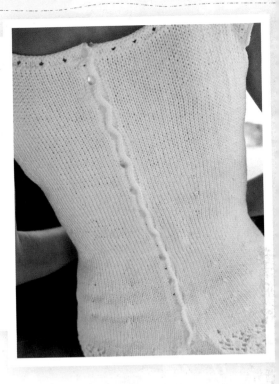

wedding
ENSEMBLE

I once saw an old photograph of a wedding gown made entirely of handknitted and crocheted laces. I was intrigued with the idea of knitting a modern-day wedding gown that would have a similar timeless quality. But I wanted to be sure that the dress could be worn for other occasions, too. Let's face it, most knitters today don't have the inclination or time to make something that would be worn only once.

stitch guide

CENTERED DOUBLE DECREASE (CDD)

RS ROWS AND ALL RNDS: Sl 2 sts as if to k2tog, k1, pass 2 slipped sts over—2 sts dec'd.

WS ROWS: Sl 2 sts as if to p2tog through the back loops, p1, pass 2 slipped sts over—2 sts dec'd.

5-INTO-1 DECREASE

Sl 2 sts as if to k2tog, k1, pass 2 slipped sts over, return st at tip of right needle to left needle and pass next 2 sts on left needle over it, then return st to right needle once more—5 sts dec'd to 1 st.

SLEEVE PATTERN (MULTIPLE OF 13 STS + 8)

ROW 1: (RS) *P2, k2, yo, ssk, p2, k2tog, yo, k1, yo, ssk; rep from * to last 8 sts, p2, k2, yo, ssk, p2.

ROW 2: K2, p4, k2, *p5, k2, p4, k2; rep from * to end.

ROW 3: *P2, k2tog, yo, k2 p2, k2tog, yo, k1, yo, ssk; rep from * to last 8 sts, p2, k2tog, yo, k2, p2.

ROW 4: Rep Row 2.

Rep Rows 1–4 for pattern.

WEDDING BELLS PATTERN (MULTIPLE OF 12 STS, DEC'D TO MULTIPLE OF 10 STS)

RNDS 1–10: *P2, k9, p1; rep from * to end.

RND 11: *P2, yo, ssk, k5, k2tog, yo, p1; rep from * to end.

RND 12: *P3, p7, p2; rep from * to end.

RND 13: *P3, yo, ssk, k3, k2tog, yo, p2; rep from * to end.

RND 14: *P4, k5, p3; rep from * to end.

RND 15: *P4, yo, ssk, k1, k2tog, yo, p3; rep from * to end.

RND 16: *P5, k3, p4; rep from * to end.

RND 17: *P5, yo, CDD (see above), yo, p4; rep from * to end.

RND 18: Purl.

RND 19: *P5, p3tog, p4; rep from * to end—patt rep has dec'd to multiple of 10 sts.

RND 20: Purl.

WORKING ROWS 9 AND 10 OF SHELLS CHART IN THE ROUND

Knit the first 3 sts of Rnd 9, *k3, yo, k1, yo, 5-into-1 dec, yo, k1, yo; rep from * to last 7 sts of Rnd 9, k3, yo, k1, yo, removing end of rnd m as you come to it work 5-into-1 dec over last 3 sts of Rnd 9 and first 2 sts of Rnd 10, replace end of rnd m after dec, yo, k1, yo, knit to end of Rnd 10.

{ make it your own }

I intentionally designed this outfit with two pieces to offer more sizing and knitting options. For each piece, choose the size that best fits your measurements for the most slimming, flattering overall look. If you don't want the wedding look, make the top alone in any color you like. Try working the front and back in a pale or neutral shade and the sleeve caps and hem lace in white—or try combining a dark neutral such as espresso or black with ecru lace. You could also knit the skirt in a different color, but be aware that you may have trouble finding different weights of yarn in the same shade. You might get around the problem by overdyeing the skirt after you knit it—but test the results on a swatch first!

{ designer notes }

I wanted to create a simple yet beautiful outfit that could be knitted in a reasonable amount of time at a reasonable cost. This skirt-and-top ensemble has the elegance of a dressmaker's fit that tapers at the waist, but it's worked in plain cotton yarns. In the skirt, the yarns progress to finer weights as they near the waist to enhance the slimming look and minimize bulk beneath the lace edging of the top. A bit of elastic at the waist helps hold up the weight of the skirt.

NOTES

¤ The lower body of the top is worked back and forth in rows in one piece to the armholes with the opening at center back. A circular needle is used to accommodate the number of stitches. The lower body is divided at the armholes for working the front and two halves of the back separately.

¤ The Shells chart pattern worked back and forth in rows for the top begins with a multiple of 10 stitches plus 1, increases to a multiple of 13 stitches plus 1 after completing Row 1, and is decreased back down to a multiple of 10 stitches plus 1 after completing Row 3. The Shells chart pattern worked in rounds for the skirt begins with a multiple of 10 stitches, increases to a multiple of 13 stitches after completing Rnd 1, and is decreased back down to a multiple of 10 stitches after completing Rnd 3.

¤ The skirt border is worked back and forth in rows, then stitches are picked up along its straight selvedge and worked upward. Each overlapping skirt tier is worked separately in the round and joined to the tier below it by working stitches from both layers together. The upper skirt is worked in the round to the beginning of the back opening, then divided for working back and forth in rows to the end of the waistband.

TOP

lower body

With B, larger cir needle, and using the long-tail method (see Glossary), CO 183 (203, 233, 263) sts. Knit 1 WS row. Establish patt from Row 1 of Shells chart (page 143) as foll: (RS) K1 (selvedge st; work in St st), work 2 sts before patt rep box once, work patt rep 17 (19, 22, 25) times, work 12 sts after patt rep box once, k1 (selvedge st; work in St st)—237 (263, 302, 341) sts (see Notes). Working selvedge

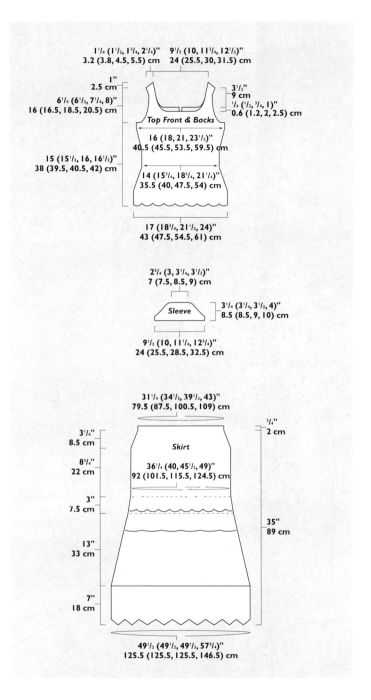

1¼ (1½, 1¾, 2¼)"
3.2 (3.8, 4.5, 5.5) cm

9½ (10, 11¾, 12½)"
24 (25.5, 30, 31.5) cm

1"
2.5 cm

3½"
9 cm

6¼ (6½, 7¼, 8)"
16 (16.5, 18.5, 20.5) cm

¼ (½, ¾, 1)"
0.6 (1.2, 2, 2.5) cm

Top Front & Backs

16 (18, 21, 23½)"
40.5 (45.5, 53.5, 59.5) cm

15 (15½, 16, 16½)"
38 (39.5, 40.5, 42) cm

14 (15¾, 18¾, 21¼)"
35.5 (40, 47.5, 54) cm

17 (18¾, 21½, 24)"
43 (47.5, 54.5, 61) cm

2¾ (3, 3¼, 3½)"
7 (7.5, 8.5, 9) cm

Sleeve

3¼ (3¼, 3½, 4)"
8.5 (8.5, 9, 10) cm

9½ (10, 11¼, 12¾)"
24 (25.5, 28.5, 32.5) cm

31¼ (34½, 39½, 43)"
79.5 (87.5, 100.5, 109) cm

¾"
2 cm

3¼"
8.5 cm

Skirt

36¼ (40, 45½, 49)"
92 (101.5, 115.5, 124.5) cm

8¾"
22 cm

3"
7.5 cm

35"
89 cm

13"
33 cm

7"
18 cm

49½ (49½, 49½, 57¾)"
125.5 (125.5, 125.5, 146.5) cm

sts in St st, cont in patt until Row 12 of chart has been completed—183 (203, 233, 263) sts rem; piece measures about 1¾" (4.5 cm) from CO. Change to MC. SET-UP ROW: (RS) K14 (16, 19, 23), place marker (pm) for inner left back dart, k14, pm for outer left back dart, k17 (20, 24, 28), pm for left side "seam," k17 (20, 24, 28), pm for outer left front dart, k14, pm for inner left front dart, k31 (35, 43, 49) for center front, pm for inner right front dart, k14, pm for outer right front dart, k17 (20, 24, 28), pm for right side "seam," k17 (20, 24, 28), pm for outer right back dart, k14, pm for inner right back dart, k14 (16, 19, 23)—93 (103, 119, 133) front sts; 45 (50, 57, 65) sts for each back; 14 sts between each pair of dart markers (m). Cont in St st, work 5 rows even in St st. DEC ROW: (RS) [Knit to 2 sts before left back dart m, k2tog, slip marker (sl m)] 2 times, knit to left side seam, sl side m, [knit to left front dart m, sl m, ssk], 2 times, [knit to 2 sts before right front dart m, k2tog, sl m] 2 times, knit to right side seam, sl side m, [knit to right back dart m, sl m, ssk] 2 times, knit to end—8 sts total dec'd, 1 st at each dart m on side of m closest to center of wearer's body. Work 7 rows even. Rep the shaping of the last 8 rows 3 more times—151 (171, 201, 231) sts rem; 77 (87, 103, 117) front sts; 37 (42, 49, 57) sts for each back. Work even until piece measures 10" (25.5 cm) from CO, ending with a WS row. INC ROW: (RS) [Knit to left back dart m, M1 (see Glossary), sl m] 2 times, knit to left side seam, sl side m, [knit to left front dart m, sl m, M1] 2 times, [knit to right front dart m, M1, sl m] 2 times, knit to right side seam, sl side m, [knit to right back dart m, sl m, M1] 2 times, knit to end—8 sts total inc'd, 1 st at each dart m on side of m closest to center of wearer's body. Work 7 rows even. Rep the shaping of the last 8 rows

2 more times—175 (195, 225, 255) sts; 89 (99, 115, 129) front sts; 43 (48, 55, 63) sts for each back. Work even until piece measures 15 (15½, 16, 16½)" (38 [39.5, 40.5, 42] cm) from CO, ending with a WS row.

left back

Removing each dart m as you come to it, k43 (48, 55, 63), remove left side m, place rem 132 (147, 170, 192) sts on holder for front and right back. Working left back sts only, BO 3 (3, 4, 4) sts at beg of next 2 WS rows, then BO 1 (2, 2, 3) st(s) at beg of foll 3 WS rows, then BO 1 st at beg of foll 4 WS rows—30 (32, 37, 42) sts rem. Work even until armhole measures 2¾ (3, 3¾, 4½)" (7 [7.5, 9.5, 11.5] cm), ending with a WS row. NEXT ROW: (RS) BO 16 (17, 20, 22) sts, knit to end—14 (15, 17, 20) sts rem. Dec 1 st at beg of next 6 (6, 7, 8) RS rows as foll: K1, k2tog, knit to end of row—8 (9, 10, 12) sts rem. Work even until armhole measures 5 (5¼, 6, 6¾)" (12.5 [13.5, 15, 17] cm), ending with a WS row. NEXT ROW: (RS) K1, ssk, knit to last 2 sts, M1, k2—no change in st count; 1 st dec'd at neck edge, 1 st inc'd at armhole edge. Work 3 rows even. Rep the last 4 rows once more, then dec 1 st at neck edge and inc 1 st at armhole edge on next RS row as before—armhole measures about 6¼ (6½, 7¼, 8)" (16 [16.5, 18.5, 20.5] cm). At shoulder edge (beg of WS rows), BO 2 (3, 4, 4) sts once, then BO 3 (3, 3, 4) sts 2 times—no sts rem.

front

Return 89 (99, 115, 129) held front sts to larger cir needle and rejoin yarn with RS facing. Removing each dart m as you come to it, BO 3 (3, 4, 4) sts, knit to end, remove right side m—86 (96, 111, 125) sts. BO 3 (3, 4, 4) sts at beg of next 3 rows, then BO 1 (2, 2, 3) st(s) at beg of next 6 rows, then BO 1 st at beg of foll 8 rows—63 (67, 79, 87) sts rem. Work even if necessary for your size until armholes measures 2½ (2½, 3, 3½)" (6.5 [6.5, 7.5, 9] cm), ending with a WS row. NEXT ROW: (RS) K16 (17, 18, 20), join new yarn and BO center 31 (33, 43, 47) sts, knit to end—16 (17, 18, 20) sts at each side. NEXT ROW: (WS) For first group of sts, purl to last 3 sts, p2tog, p1; for next group of sts, p1, ssp (see Glossary), purl to end—1 st dec'd at each neck edge. NEXT ROW: (RS) For first group of sts, knit to last 3, ssk, k1; for next group of sts, k1, k2tog, knit to end—1 sts dec'd at each neck edge. Rep the last 2 rows 3 more times—8 (9, 10, 12) sts rem at each side. Work even until armhole measures 5 (5¼, 6, 6¾)" (12.5 [13.5, 15, 17] cm), ending with a WS row. NEXT ROW: (RS) For first group of sts, k2, M1, k1, knit to last 3 sts, k2tog, k1; for next group of sts, k1, ssk, knit to last 2 sts, M1, k2—no change in st count; 1 st dec'd at each neck edge, 1 st inc'd at each armhole edge. Work 3 rows even. Rep the last 4 rows once more, then dec 1 at each neck edge and inc 1 at each armhole edge on next RS row as before—armhole measures about 6¼ (6½, 7¼, 8)" (16 [16.5, 18.5, 20.5] cm). At each armhole edge, BO 2 (3, 4, 4) sts once, then BO 3 (3, 3, 4) sts 2 times—no sts rem.

right back

Return 43 (48, 55, 63) held back sts to larger cir needle and rejoin yarn with RS facing. Removing each dart m as you come to it, BO 3 (3, 4, 4) sts, knit to end—40 (45, 51, 59) sts rem. BO 3 (3, 4, 4) sts at beg of next RS row, then BO 1 (2, 2, 3) st(s) at beg of foll 3 RS rows, then BO 1 st at beg of foll 4 RS rows—30 (32, 37, 42) sts rem. Work even until armhole measures 2¾ (3, 3¾, 4½)" (7 [7.5, 9.5, 11.5] cm), ending with a RS row. NEXT ROW: (WS) BO 16 (17, 20, 22) sts, purl to end—14 (15, 17, 20) sts rem. Dec 1 st at end of next 6 (6, 7, 8) RS rows as foll: Knit to last 3 sts, ssk, k1—8 (9, 10, 12) sts rem. Work even until armhole measures 5 (5¼, 6, 6¾)" (12.5 [13.5, 15, 17] cm), ending with a WS row. NEXT ROW: (RS) K2, M1, knit to last 3 sts, k2tog, k1—no change in st count; 1 st dec'd at neck edge, 1 st inc'd at armhole edge. Work 3 rows even. Rep the last 4 rows once more, then dec 1 st at neck edge and inc 1 st at armhole edge on next RS row as before—armhole measures about 6¼ (6½, 7¼, 8)" (16 [16.5, 18.5, 20.5] cm). At shoulder edge (beg of RS rows), BO 2 (3, 4, 4) sts once, then BO 3 (3, 3, 4) sts 2 times—no sts rem.

SLEEVES (MAKE 2)

With A, smaller straight needles, and using the long-tail method, CO 68 (70, 80, 90) sts. Beg with a RS row, knit 2 rows, then work 2 rows in St st. NEXT ROW: (RS) K2tog, k1 (0, 1, 0), *k2, yo, ssk; rep from * to last 5 (4, 5, 4) sts, k2 (3, 2, 3), ssk—66 (68, 78, 88) sts rem. Purl 1 WS row. NEXT ROW: (RS) K2tog, k1, *yo, ssk; rep from * to last 3 sts, k1, ssk—64 (66, 76, 86) sts rem. NEXT ROW: (WS) P2, *yo, p2tog; rep from * to last 2 sts, p2. Knit 2 rows. NEXT ROW: (RS) K2tog, knit to last 2 sts, ssk—62 (64, 74, 84) sts rem. Purl 1 WS row, dec 0 (0, 1, 1) st in center—62 (64, 73, 83) sts; piece measures about ¾" (2 cm) from CO. Establish sleeve patt (see Stitch Guide) on next row as foll: (RS) K1 (2, 0, 5), work Row 1 of sleeve patt over center 60 (60, 73, 73) sts, k1 (2, 0, 5). NOTE: If during shaping there are not enough stitches to work a decrease with its companion yarnover, work the stitches in stockinette instead to avoid throwing off the stitch

Shells

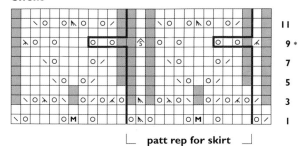

⌐ patt rep for skirt ⌐

*See Stitch Guide for working Rows 9 and 10 in the rnd.

	k on RS; p on WS
·	p on RS; k on WS
O	yo on both RS and WS
/	k2tog on RS; p2tog on WS
\	ssk on RS; ssp on WS (see Glossary)
⋏	k3tog
⋋	sssk on RS; sssp on WS (see Glossary)
⋌	sl 1, k2tog, psso
⋀	centered double dec (see Stitch Guide)
⑤	5-into-1 dec (see Stitch Guide)
M	M1 (see Glossary)
▓	no stitch
☐	pattern repeat

Shetland Lace

65
63
61
59
57
55
53
51
49
47
45
43
41
39
37
35
33
31
29
27
25
23
21
19
17
15
13
11
9
7
5
3
1

144

count. Working sts at each side of sleeve patt in St st, work Row 2 of patt. Beg on the next RS row (Row 3 of patt), dec 1 st each end of needle every 4 rows 3 times by working k2tog at beg of row and ssk at end of row—56 (58, 67, 77) sts rem. Dec 1 st each side on the next 6 (6, 10, 14) rows, dec on RS rows as before, and dec on WS rows by working ssp at beg of row and p2tog at end of row—44 (46, 47, 49) sts rem. BO 3 sts at beg of next 2 rows, then BO 4 sts at beg of foll 2 rows, then BO 5 sts at beg of foll 2 rows—20 (22, 23, 25) sts rem; piece measures about 3¼ (3¼, 3½, 4)" (8.5 [8.5, 9, 10] cm) from CO. BO all sts.

FINISHING

Block pieces to measurements. With MC threaded on a tapestry needle, sew backs to front at shoulders.

buttonband

With B, larger straight needles, RS facing, and beg at start of right back neck shaping, pick up and knit 107 (112, 117, 127) sts along right back edge, ending at first row of MC in lower body; do not pick up any sts from selvedge of shell patt. Beg with a WS row, knit 2 rows, purl 1 WS row, then knit the next 2 rows. BO all sts.

buttonhole band

With B, larger straight needles, RS facing, and beg at first row of MC in lower body, pick up and knit 107 (112, 117, 127) sts along left back edge, ending at start of left back neck shaping; do not pick up any sts from selvedge of shell patt. Beg with a WS row, knit 2 rows. BUTTONHOLE ROW: (WS) P2, *yo, p2tog, p3; rep from * to end—21 (22, 23, 25) eyelet holes completed. Knit 2 rows. BO all sts.

neck trim

With B, smaller cir needle, RS facing, and beg at BO edge of buttonhole band, pick up and knit 49 (52, 61, 65) sts along left back neck to left shoulder seam, 86 (90, 107, 114) sts along front neck to right shoulder seam, and 49 (52, 61, 65) sts along right back neck to end at BO edge of buttonband—184 (194, 229, 244) sts total. Knit 2 rows, ending with a RS row. EYELET ROW: (WS) P1, p2tog, yo, *p3, yo, p2tog; rep from * to last st, end p1. Knit 2 rows. With RS facing, BO all sts.

seams

Sew selvedges of sleeve caps into armholes, matching center of each sleeve cap to shoulder seam; sleeve caps extend only partway down the armholes. For unfinished armhole edges, turn raw edge under ¼" (6 mm) to WS at base of armhole, tapering to ⅛" (3 mm) at ends of sleeve cap, and sew in place on WS.

Weave in loose ends. Block garment with damp cloth and iron as necessary, carefully blocking out lace patterns of lower edge and sleeves. With sharp-point sewing needle and thread, sew the highest button to right back neck trim, opposite eyelet hole closest to the edge in left back neck trim. To attach rem buttons, skip the highest eyelet hole in buttonhole band, and starting with the 2nd eyelet hole down from the top, sew rem 10 (11, 11, 12) buttons to buttonband opposite every other eyelet hole, leaving bottom 1 (0, 1, 1) eyelet hole without a button.

Border

Chart rows labeled (right side): 1, 3, 5, 7, 9, 11, 13, 15, 17

Legend:

- ☐ k on RS; p on WS
- · p on RS; k on WS
- ○ yo on both RS and WS
- ╱ k2tog on RS; p2tog on WS
- ╲ ssk on RS; ssp on WS (see Glossary)
- ⊼ k3tog
- ⋏ sssk on RS; sssp on WS (see Glossary)
- ⋏ sl 1, k2tog, psso
- ⋀ centered double dec (see Stitch Guide)
- ⥮ 5-into-1 dec (see Stitch Guide)
- M M1 (see Glossary)
- ▪ no stitch
- ☐ pattern repeat

SKIRT
lace underskirt

With A, second-largest needle, and using the long-tail method (see Glossary), CO 35 sts. Rep Rows 1–18 of Border chart 18 (18, 18, 21) times—324 (324, 324, 378) patt rows completed; piece measures about 49½ (49½, 49½, 57¾)" (125.5 [125.5, 125.5, 146.5] cm) from CO. With RS facing, BO all sts. Turn border sideways with RS facing so that straight selvedge is at the top, and rejoin A to righthand edge, ready to pick up sts across straight top edge. With second-largest needle and RS facing, pick up and knit 307 (307, 307, 361) sts across straight selvedge of lower border (about 17 sts for each patt rep of border). With RS still facing, place marker (pm) and join for working in rnds. Knit 2 rnds. Establish patt from Rnd 1 of Shetland Lace chart as foll: Work 18 sts before patt rep box once, work 54-st patt rep 5 (5, 5, 6) times, work 19 sts after patt rep box once. Work even until Row 66 of chart has been completed—piece measures about 17½" (44.5 cm) from deepest point of lower border. Work even in St st until piece measures 19½" (49.5 cm) from deepest point of lower border. NEXT RND: K1 (1, 1, 3), *k2tog, k2; rep from * to last 2 sts, k2—231 (231, 231, 272) sts. Knit 1 rnd. NEXT RND: Knit, dec 61 (51, 21, 52) sts evenly—170 (180, 210, 220) sts rem. Work even if necessary until piece measures 20" (51 cm) from deepest point of lower border. Cut yarn and leave sts on needle.

wedding bells tier

With C, largest cir needle, and using the long-tail method, CO 204 (216, 252, 264) sts. Pm and join for working in rnds, being careful not to twist sts. Work Rnds 1–20 of wedding bells patt (see Stitch Guide)—170 (180, 210, 220) sts rem; piece measures about 3¼" (8.5 cm) from CO. Leave sts on needle, but do not cut yarn.

join tiers

Slip wedding bells tier down from the top and over the lace underskirt. Hold needles with live sts tog and parallel, with lace underskirt needle behind wedding bells needle. With RS facing and C, use tip of largest cir needle to work k2tog (1 st from each needle) all the way around to join the 2 layers—170 (180, 210, 220) sts rem on largest cir. With C and largest needle, work even in St st until assembled piece measures 23" (58.5 cm) from deepest point of lower border. NEXT RND: Knit 1 rnd, inc 30 (40, 40, 50) sts evenly spaced—200 (220, 250, 270) sts. Cut yarn and place sts on second-largest needle for holder.

upper skirt

With B, largest cir needle, and using the long-tail method, CO 200 (220, 250, 270) sts. Pm and join for working in rnds, being careful not to twist sts. Purl 1 rnd. Establish patt from Shells chart by working Rnd 1 of patt rep marked for skirt 20 (22, 25, 27) times around—260 (286, 325, 351) sts (see Notes). Cont in patt, work Rnds 2–12 once (see Stitch Guide for working Rnds 9 and 10), then rep Rnds 1–12 once more—200 (220, 250, 270) sts rem. Knit 2 rnds—piece measures about 3¾" (9.5 cm) from CO. Cut yarn and leave sts on needle.

join tiers

Slip shell patt down from the top and over the wedding bells tier. Hold needles with live sts tog and parallel, with wedding bells needle behind shell patt needle. Join MC to beg of rnd with RS facing, and use tip of largest cir needle to work k2tog (1 st from each needle) all the way around to join the 2 layers—200 (220, 250, 270) sts rem on largest cir needle. With MC, work in St st until piece measures 31¾" (80.5 cm) from deepest point of lower border and about 8¾" (22 cm) from last joining rnd, or 3¼" (8.5 cm) less than desired length, ending last rnd 2 sts before end of rnd m.

shape waist and back opening

Change to B and second-smallest needle. SET-UP ROW: K2 (last 2 sts of previous rnd), remove end of rnd m, k2, pm for buttonhole band, knit to end, pm, use the backward-loop method (see Glossary) to CO 4 sts for buttonband—204 (224, 254, 274) sts. Change to working back and forth in rows and work 1 WS row as foll: [P1, k1] 2 times, slip marker (sl m), purl to last 4 sts, sl m, [k1, p1] 2 times.

ROW 1: (RS, buttonhole row) K1, [yo, k2tog] for buttonhole, p1, sl m, knit to last 4 sts, [p1, k1] 2 times.

ROWS 2, 4, AND 6: [P1, k1] 2 times, sl m, purl to last 4 sts, sl m, [k1, p1] 2 times.

ROWS 3 AND 5: [K1, p1] 2 times, sl m, knit to last 4 sts, sl m, [p1, k1] 2 times.

ROW 7: (buttonhole and dec row) K1, [yo, k2tog] for buttonhole, p1, sl m, k23 (26, 29, 32), ssk, pm for left back dart, k25 (27, 31, 34), pm for left side "seam," k25 (27, 31, 34), pm for left front dart, k2tog, k46 (52, 60, 62) for center front, ssk, pm for right front dart, k25 (27, 31, 34), pm for right side "seam," k25 (27, 31, 34), pm for right back dart, k2tog, k19 (22, 25, 28), sl m, [p1, k1] 2 times—200 (220, 250, 270) sts; 98 (108, 124, 132) front sts, 53 (58, 65, 71) left back sts including 4-st buttonhole band, 49 (54, 61, 67) right back sts. Sl each dart and side m as you come to it on foll rows.

ROW 8: Change to smallest needle and Rep Row 2.

ROWS 9 AND 11: Rep Row 3.

EVEN-NUMBERED ROWS 10–24: Rep Row 2.

ROW 13: (buttonhole and dec row) K1, [yo, k2tog] for buttonhole, sl m, knit to 2 sts before left back dart m, ssk, sl m, knit to left front dart m, sl m, k2tog, knit to 2 sts before right front dart m, ssk, sl m, knit to right back dart m, sl m, k2tog, knit to last 4 sts, sl m, [p1, k1] 2 times—4 sts dec'd, 2 sts inside front dart m, 1 st on inner side of each back dart m.

ROWS 15 AND 17: Rep Row 3.

ROW 19: (buttonhole and dec row) Rep Row 13—192 (212, 242, 262) sts rem; 94 (104, 120, 128) front sts, 51 (56, 63, 69) left back sts, 47 (52, 59, 65) right back sts.

ROWS 21 AND 23: Rep Row 3.

ROW 25: (buttonhole row) Rep Row 1.

ROW 26: Rep Row 2—waist section measures about 3¼" (8.5 cm) from start of back opening; piece measures about 35" (89 cm) from deepest point of lower border.

Working 4 sts at each end of row in established rib and rem sts in St st, work 5 rows even. Knit across next WS row for fold line. Work all sts in St st for 5 rows. BO all sts.

FINISHING

Turn waistband to WS along fold line and sew in place with B threaded on a tapestry needle. With B threaded on a tapestry needle, sew 4 CO sts at base of buttonband extension to WS behind buttonhole band. Weave in loose ends. Steam-block to measurements under a damp towel, stretching lace patterns as necessary to achieve the desired amount of openness. Thread elastic through waistband and adjust length to where best fit is achieved; try to minimize the amount of gathering at the waist to avoid a bulky appearance. With sharp-point sewing needle and thread, secure each end of elastic just inside waistband edge on either side of back opening. With B threaded on a tapestry needle, sew ends of elastic casing closed. Sew buttons to ribbed buttonband, opposite buttonholes.

GLOSSARY

abbreviations

beg	begin(s); beginning	*rep*	repeat(s); repeating
BO	bind off	*rev St st*	reverse stockinette stitch
CC	contrast color	*rnd(s)*	round(s)
cm	centimeter(s)	*RS*	right side
cn	cable needle	*sl*	slip
CO	cast on	*sl st*	slip st (slip 1 stitch purlwise unless otherwise indicated)
cont	continue(s); continuing		
dec(s)	decrease(s); decreasing	*ssk*	slip 2 stitches knitwise, one at a time, from the left needle to right needle, insert left needle tip through both front loops and knit together from this position (1 stitch decrease)
dpn	double-pointed needles		
foll	follow(s); following		
g	gram(s)		
inc(s)	increase(s); increasing		
k	knit		
k1f&b	knit into the front and back of same stitch	*st(s)*	stitch(es)
		St st	stockinette stitch
kwise	knitwise, as if to knit	*tbl*	through back loop
m	marker(s)	*tog*	together
MC	main color	*WS*	wrong side
mm	millimeter(s)	*wyb*	with yarn in back
M1	make one (increase)	*wyf*	with yarn in front
p	purl	*yd*	yard(s)
p1f&b	purl into front and back of same stitch	*yo*	yarnover
		*	repeat starting point
patt(s)	pattern(s)	**	repeat all instructions between asterisks
psso	pass slipped stitch over	( )	alternate measurements and/or instructions
pwise	purlwise, as if to purl		
rem	remain(s); remaining	[ ]	work instructions as a group a specified number of times

BUTTONHOLES

one-row buttonhole

Bring the yarn to the front of the work, slip the next stitch purlwise, then return the yarn to the back. *Slip the next stitch, pass the second stitch over the slipped stitch (Figure 1) and drop it off the needle. Repeat from * 3 more times. Slip the last stitch on the right needle to the left needle and turn the work around. Bring the working yarn to the back, [insert the right needle between the first and second stitches on the left needle (Figure 2), draw up a loop and place it on the left needle] 5 times. Turn the work around. With the yarn in back, slip the first stitch and pass the extra cast-on stitch over it (Figure 3) and off the needle to complete the buttonhole.

CAST-ONS

backward-loop cast-on

*Loop working yarn and place it on needle backward so that it doesn't unwind. Repeat from *.

cable cast-on

Hold needle with working yarn in your left hand with the wrong side of the work facing you. *Insert right needle between the first two stitches on left needle (Figure 1), wrap yarn around needle as if to knit, draw yarn through (Figure 2), and place new loop on left needle (Figure 3) to form a new stitch. Repeat from * for the desired number of stitches, always working between the first two stitches on the left needle.

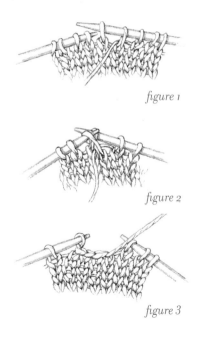

figure 1

figure 2

figure 3

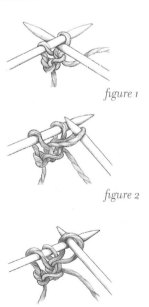

figure 1

figure 2

figure 3

long-tail (continental) cast-on

Leaving a long tail (about ½" [1.3 cm] for each stitch to be cast on), make a slipknot and place on right needle. Place thumb and index finger of your left hand between the yarn ends so that working yarn is around your index finger and tail end is around your thumb and secure the yarn ends with your other fingers. Hold your palm upwards, making a V of yarn (Figure 1). *Bring needle up through loop on thumb (Figure 2), catch first strand around index finger, and go back down through loop on thumb (Figure 3). Drop loop off thumb and, placing thumb back in V configuration, tighten resulting stitch on needle (Figure 4). Repeat from * for the desired number of stitches.

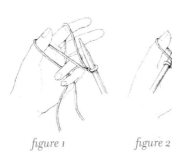

figure 1

figure 2

figure 3 *figure 4*

CROCHET

crochet chain (ch)

Make a slipknot and place it on crochet hook if there isn't a loop already on the hook. *Yarn over hook and draw through loop on hook. Repeat from * for the desired number of stitches. To fasten off, cut yarn and draw end through last loop formed.

reverse single crochet

Working from left to right, insert hook into a stitch, draw through a loop, bring yarn over hook, and draw it through the first loop. *Insert hook into next stitch to the right (Figure 1), draw through a loop, bring yarn over hook again (Figure 2), and draw a loop through both loops on hook (Figure 3). Repeat from * for the desired number of stitches.

figure 1

figure 2 *figure 3*

single crochet (sc)

*Insert hook into the second chain from the hook (or the next stitch), yarn over hook and draw through a loop, yarn over hook (Figure 1), and draw it through both loops on hook (Figure 2). Repeat from * for the desired number of stitches.

figure 1

figure 2

slip-stitch crochet (sl st)

*Insert hook into stitch, yarn over hook and draw a loop through both the stitch and the loop already on hook. Repeat from * for the desired number of stitches.

DECREASES

slip, slip, knit (ssk)

Slip two stitches individually knitwise (Figure 1), insert left needle tip into the front of these two slipped stitches, and use the right needle to knit them together through their back loops (Figure 2).

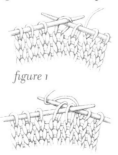

figure 1

figure 2

slip, slip, slip, knit (sssk)

Slip three stitches individually knitwise (Figure 1), insert left needle tip into the front of these three slipped stitches, and use the right needle to knit them together through their back loops (Figure 2).

figure 1

figure 2

slip, slip, purl (ssp)

Holding yarn in front, slip two stitches individually knitwise (Figure 1), then slip these two stitches back onto left needle (they will be turned on the needle) and purl them together through their back loops (Figure 2).

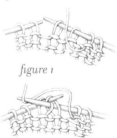

figure 1

figure 2

slip, slip, slip, purl (sssp)

Work as for ssp (above), but slip three stitches individually, then purl them together through their back loops.

EMBROIDERY

backstitch

* Insert thread needle at the right edge of the right side of a stitch then bring it back out at the left side of a stitch two stitches away. Insert the needle again between the first two stitches and bring it out two stitches away. Repeat from *.

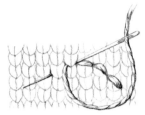

daisy stitch

*Bring threaded needle out of knitted background from back to front, form a short loop and insert needle into background where it came out. Keeping the loop under the needle, bring the needle back out of the background a short distance away (Figure 1), pull loop snug, and insert needle into fabric on far side of loop. Beginning each stitch at the same point in the background, repeat from * for the desired number of petals (Figure 2; six petals shown).

figure 1

figure 2

running stitch

Bring threaded needle in and out of background to form a dashed line.

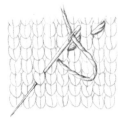

GRAFTING

kitchener stitch

Arrange stitches on two needles so that there is the same number of stitches on each needle. Hold the needles parallel to each other with wrong sides of the knitting together. Allowing about ½" (1.3 cm) per stitch to be grafted, thread matching yarn on a tapestry needle. Work from right to left as follows:

STEP 1. Bring tapestry needle through the first stitch on the front needle as if to purl and leave the stitch on the needle (Figure 1).

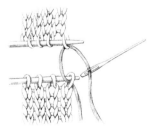

figure 1

STEP 2. Bring tapestry needle through the first stitch on the back needle as if to knit and leave that stitch on the needle (Figure 2).

STEP 3. Bring tapestry needle through the first front stitch as if to knit and slip this stitch off the needle, then bring tapestry needle through the next front stitch as if to purl and leave this stitch on the needle (Figure 3).

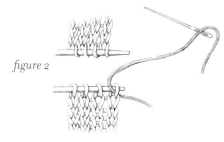

figure 2

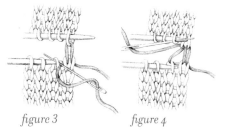

figure 3   *figure 4*

STEP 4. Bring tapestry needle through the first back stitch as if to purl and slip this stitch off the needle, then bring tapestry needle through the next back stitch as if to knit and leave this stitch on the needle (Figure 4).

Repeat Steps 3 and 4 until one stitch remains on each needle, adjusting the tension to match the rest of the knitting as you go. To finish, bring tapestry needle through the front stitch as if to knit and slip this stitch off the needle, then bring tapestry needle through the back stitch as if to purl and slip this stitch off the needle.

I-CORD
(ALSO CALLED KNIT-CORD)

Using two double-pointed needles, cast on the desired number of stitches (usually three to four). *Without turning the needle, slide stitches to other end of needle, pull the yarn around the back, and knit the stitches as usual. Repeat from * for desired length.

INCREASES

bar increase (k1f&b)
Knit into a stitch but leave it on the left needle (Figure 1), then knit through the back loop of the same stitch (Figure 2) and slip the original stitch off the needle (Figure 3).

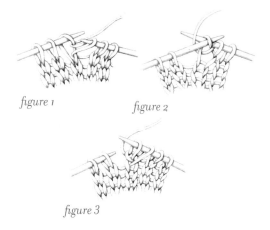

figure 1   *figure 2*

figure 3

raised make one—left slant (M1L)

NOTE: Use the left slant if no direction of slant is specified.

With left needle tip, lift the strand between the last knitted stitch and the first stitch on the left needle from front to back (Figure 1), then knit the lifted loop through the back (Figure 2).

figure 1

figure 2

raised make one—right slant (M1R)

With left needle tip, lift the strand between the needles from back to front (Figure 1). Knit the lifted loop through the front (Figure 2).

figure 1

figure 2

raised make one purlwise (M1 pwise)

With left needle tip, lift the strand between the needles from back to front (Figure 1), then purl the lifted loop through the front (Figure 2).

figure 1

figure 2

P1f&b

Purl into a stitch but leave it on the left needle (Figure 1), then purl through the back loop of the same stitch (Figure 2) and slip the original stitch off the needle.

figure 1

figure 2

SEAMS

invisible horizontal seam

Working with the bound-off edges opposite each other, right sides of the knitting facing you, and working into the stitches just below the bound-off edges, bring threaded tapestry needle out at the center of the first stitch (i.e., go under half of the first stitch) on one side of the seam, then bring needle in and out under the first whole stitch on the other side (Figure 1). *Bring needle into the center of the same stitch it came out of before, then out in the center of the adjacent stitch (Figure 2). Bring needle in and out under the next whole stitch on the other side (Figure 3). Repeat from *, ending with a half-stitch on the first side.

SHORT-ROWS

short-rows knit side

Work to turning point, slip next stitch purlwise (Figure 1), bring the yarn to the front, then slip the same stitch back to the left needle (Figure 2), turn the work around and bring the yarn in position for the next stitch—one stitch has been wrapped and the yarn is correctly positioned to work the next stitch. When you come to a wrapped stitch on a subsequent row, hide the wrap by working it together with the wrapped stitch as follows: Insert right needle tip under the wrap (from the front if wrapped stitch is a knit stitch; from the back if wrapped stitch is a purl stitch; Figure 3), then into the stitch on the needle, and work the stitch and its wrap together as a single stitch.

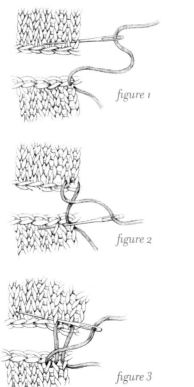

figure 1

figure 2

figure 3

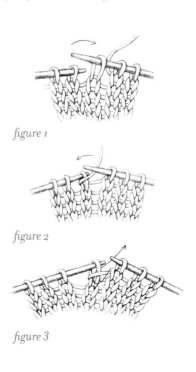

figure 1

figure 2

figure 3

short-rows purl side

Work to the turning point, slip the next stitch purlwise to the right needle, bring the yarn to the back of the work (Figure 1), return the slipped stitch to the left needle, bring the yarn to the front between the needles (Figure 2), and turn the work so that the knit side is facing—one stitch has been wrapped and the yarn is correctly positioned to knit the next stitch. To hide the wrap on a subsequent purl row, work to the wrapped stitch, use the tip of the right needle to pick up the wrap from the back, place it on the left needle (Figure 3), then purl it together with the wrapped stitch.

ZIPPER

With right side facing and zipper closed, pin zipper to the knitted pieces so edges cover the zipper teeth. With contrasting thread and right side facing, baste zipper in place close to teeth (Figure 1). Turn work over and with matching sewing thread and needle, stitch outer edges of zipper to wrong side of knitting (Figure 2), being careful to follow a single column of stitches in the knitting to keep zipper straight. Turn work back to right side facing and with matching sewing thread, sew knitted fabric close to teeth (Figure 3). Remove basting.

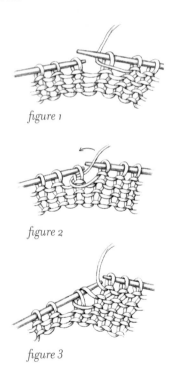

figure 1

figure 2

figure 3

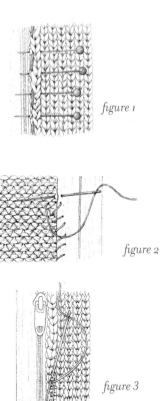

figure 1

figure 2

figure 3

bibliography

There are dozens of helpful books on the market for knitwear designers. The ones listed below are some that I find myself reaching for time and again. This is by no means a complete list—visit your local bookstore or yarn shop for many more resources.

Eichenseer, Erika, Erika Grill, and Betta Krön. *Oma's Strickgeheimnisse: 200 Bezaubernde Muster*. Rosenheimer Verlagshaus Gmbh & Co. KG, Rosenheim, 2000.

Michelson, Carmen, and Mary-Ann Davis. *The Knitter's Guide To Sweater Design*. Loveland, Colorado: Interweave Press, 1989.

Miller, Sharon. *Heirloom Knitting*. Gremista, Lerwick: The Shetland Times Ltd., 2002.

Newton, Deborah. *Designing Knitwear*. Newtown, Connecticut: Taunton Press, 1998.

Phillips, Mary Walker. *Creative Knitting*. St Paul, Minnesota: Dos Tejedoras, 1986.

——. *Knitting Counterpanes*. Newtown, Connecticut: Taunton Press, 1989.

Stanfield, Lesley. *The New Stitch Library*. Radnor, Pennsylvania: Chilton Book Company, 1992.

Vogue Knitting magazine. *Vogue Knitting*. New York: Pantheon Books, 1989.

Walker, Barbara G. *A Treasury of Knitting Patterns*, *A Second Treasury of Knitting Patterns*, and *A Third Treasury of Knitting Patterns*. Pittsville, Wisconsin: Schoolhouse Press, 1998.

Croquis templates:
Kimball, Carol. *Fashion Sketching for Any Body*. Lyons, Colorado: PO Box 546, Lyons, CO 80540, 2003. (csquarew@concentric.net)

Computer Charting Software:
Stitch Painter by Cochenille Design at cochenille.com.
Knit Visualizer by Knit Foundry at knitfoundry.com.

sources for supplies

Berroco Inc.
PO Box 367
14 Elmdale Rd.
Uxbridge, MA 01569
www.berroco.com
In Canada: S. R. Kertzer Ltd.
    Cotton Twist
    Lang Lurex
    Touche

Blue Sky Alpacas Inc.
PO Box 88
Cedar, MN 55011
www.blueskyalpacas.com
    Handdyed Worsted

Classic Elite Yarns
122 Western Ave.
Lowell, MA 01851
www.classiceliteyarns.com
    Premiere

Design Source/
Manos Del Uruguay
PO Box 770
Medford, MA 02155
    Handdyed Wool

DMC Inc.
77 S. Hackensack Ave.
Port Kearny, Bldg. 10F
S. Kearny NJ 07032
Baroque Crochet Cotton Size 10
    Size 5 Pearl Cotton

Diamond Yarn
9697 St. Laurent, Ste. 101
Montreal, QC
Canada H3L 2N1
and
115 Martin Ross, Unit 3
Toronto, ON
Canada M3J 2L9
www.diamondyarn.com

Fiesta Yarns
5401 San Diego NE
Albuquerque, NM 87113
www.fiestayarns.com
    La Luz

JCA, Inc./
Adrienne Vittadini/
Reynolds
35 Scales Ln.
Townsend, MA 01469
www.jcacrafts.com
    Adrienne Vittadini Celia
    Reynolds Andean Alpaca Regal

Knit One, Crochet Too Inc.
91 Tandberg Trl., Unit 6
Windham, ME 04062
www.knitonecrochettoo.com
    Ambrosia
    Douceur et Soie

M & J Trimming
1008 Sixth Ave.
New York, NY 10018
www.mjtrim.com

Muench Yarns Inc./GGH
1323 Scott St.
Petaluma CA 94954-1135
www.muenchyarns.com
In Canada: Oberlyn Yarns
    Scarlett

Oberlyn Yarns
5640 Rue Valcourt
Brossard, QC
Canada J4W 1C5
www.oberlyn.ca

Skacel/Schoeller Stahl
PO Box 88110
Seattle, WA 98138
www.skacelknitting.com
    Schoeller Stahl Palma

S.R. Kertzer Ltd.
6060 Burnside Ct., Unit 2
Mississauga, ON
Canada
L5T 2T5
www.kertzer.com

Tahki Stacy Charles Inc.
70–30 80th St., Bldg. 36
Ridgewood, NY 11385
www.tahkistacycharles.com
In Canada: Diamond Yarn
    Baby
    Donegal
    Tweed
    Torino

Westminster Fibers
Rowan
165 Ledge St.
Nashua, NH 03060
www.westminsterfibers.com
In Canada: Diamond Yarn
    Rowan Cotton Glace
    Rowan Kidsilk Haze
    Rowan Lurex Shimmer
    Rowan Silk Tweed

index